RECIPES FOR SUCCESS

RECIPES FOR SUCCESS

ROSAMOND CARDIGAN

The Crowood Press

First published in 1988 by
The Crowood Press
Ramsbury, Marlborough,
Wiltshire SN8 2HE

British Library Cataloguing in Publication Data
Cardigan, Rosamond
    Recipes for success.
    1. Food. Dishes for special occasions –
    Recipes
    I. Title
    641.5'68

    ISBN 1–85223–083–5

For David, Thomas and Catherine

Line illustrations by Alex Clinton.

Typeset by Q-Set, 2 Conway Road, Hucclecote, Gloucester.
Printed in Great Britain by Billing & Sons, Worcester

CONTENTS

	Acknowledgements	6
	Introduction	7
1	Soups	12
2	Hors-d'Oeuvres	20
3	Pasta	48
4	Eggs	54
5	Fish	62
6	Game	82
7	Traditional Luncheon and Nursery Puddings	96
8	Just Desserts for Dinner Parties	120
9	Quick and Rich Desserts	153
10	Tea-Time	164
11	Accompaniments	172
	Glossary	175
	Index	176

ACKNOWLEDGEMENTS

In some books one reads how the author sat in the kitchen watching the cook or her mother prepare food, of how they were allowed to stir the soup, make cakes or fudge. My mother would freely admit that when she was first married she could not boil the proverbial egg and she struggled for years with the Wagnerian dramas that burst from her oven. I am certain that is why I was sent to Tante Marie!

My cooking owes a great deal to the marvellous teaching at Tante Marie and some of the recipes come from their books. Otherwise the collection has been added to by recipes from friends, which have been subtly changed and passed about until I added them to this book.

My thanks, also, to Margaret Clark for typing the manuscript.

INTRODUCTION

This is a collection of 150 or so of my favourite recipes and most of them aim at speed and simplicity. This is not a book for expert cooks but for those of average ability who enjoy cooking and entertaining and who lead busy lives. Many of the recipes can be prepared in advance and re-heated, and some require little or no cooking at all. Presentation is important – improvise and use your imagination when decorating dishes. The starter or hors-d'oeuvre is particularly important because very often it sets the style of the lunch or dinner.

Friends are always asking me for suggestions and so I have collated here a selection of ideas for lunches, teas, dinner parties and informal suppers. There are literally millions of books, specialist magazines and articles in the daily newspapers published about food and cooking, and it is a seemingly bottomless pit, as interest in all matters culinary never seems to wane. But not everyone has the time or inclination to test for themselves the most successful and appealing recipes. Thus, this book represents a compilation of my own knowledge made up from various classical French and other recipes. (I only hope that there aren't too many great chefs turning in their graves!) Many recipes have been swapped with friends, recipes which, no doubt, originated in many different places and have been altered and adapted in sort of culinary Chinese whispers.

I am often accused by my husband of spending too much time 'indulging' myself (his words) by talking to those he refers to as my 'old ladies', who tell me stories of days gone by. I have had many conversations with the old family cook. There we would sit in her cottage beside her glowing fire, with some tea sweetened with condensed milk and a slice or two of home-made cake, and over a period of time she told me many snippets about her life and times as cook to my husband's grandfather and family. I decided that in some small way she should be immortalised in print and that her wealth of knowledge should not be lost.

There were many reminiscences of life below stairs at Tottenham House, the vast family home of my husband, set in parkland laid out by Capability Brown and surrounded by the only private forest in England. These stories were handed on to her by her own parents and their friends who had worked there and on the estate. First-hand she told of her own life as daughter of the Head Forester – sketches that built up a picture and social history of all their doings. We pored over old recipe books and cuttings from the weekly women's journals of the time which were often sandwiched between beauty tips for careworn hands (rub together sugar and oil) or for aching feet (mustard and herbs) – both so important to a cook!

Unlike us, with our modern kitchens and every conceivable gadget, she managed to cook on the smallest range known to man (it still exists) and produced enormous meals for large numbers of people whenever there were shooting lunches or weekend house-parties. Butter was churned from milk from the home farm, and nothing whatsoever was bought in. Indeed, the idea of such modern kitchen staples as ready-cooked and frozen meats and fish in sauces, shop cakes and biscuits would produce a look of shock and horror on her normally mildly anxious face – an anxious expression probably caused by too many years worrying about the rise and fall of soufflés or the tenderness of her venison cutlets. I expect the same will happen to me.

I was allowed to call her Binty, just as that certain generation of small boys did who were unable to pronounce her name correctly, which was Vincent. She was, as the then Countess of Cardigan described her, 'an inspired cook'. Binty's mother had been in service as a cook and had taught her the basic rules. However, it was not until after the Second World War that her real abilities were recognised and she came to work for the Cardigans.

Binty told me that she considered presentation was very important, but later said that she spent no time at all decorating food. The fabulous china and silver plates they ate from probably helped to create a beautiful impression with the food arranged simply. She described to me delicate silver baskets filled with red, black and white currants that had been crystallised in sugar. The centre-piece on the dining-room table was piled high with caramelised, cream-filled profiteroles, with crystallised strawberries peering through the gaps. No doubt the ancestors hanging on the walls gazed hungrily down upon the feast.

Descriptions of those peaceful days, when family meals were more of a ritual, are far removed from our hectic attempts at running the household smoothly. Sadly, no one remembers the whereabouts of Binty's recipe books, although the recipes would undoubtedly need some updating since tastes and fashions change considerably in 30 or 40 years. However, she did give me many of her favourite recipes and all that she could remember of the grand dinner party menus on which she worked. I have added some of these suggestions to my own collection stored in a scruffy notebook, and have deciphered them for inclusion in this book. I have also collected some of the outstanding dishes from restaurants visited and many other varied ideas have all been scribbled in.

Binty, having begun as a lady's maid in the 1920s, was still making the occasional rook pie or strawberry tart in the 1980s. When I first met my husband, he claimed to have cooked an entire dinner party in my honour. It was only several years later that I discovered Binty had been coaxed out of retirement to create an impressive dinner for the new girlfriend!

As far as my own culinary philosophy is concerned, I would far rather eat two starters and a pudding, and forego my main course. By increasing the quantities of ingredients in many of the recipes in this book, it is possible to make an extremely delicious main course. It is very important to read a recipe right through to the end so that you are sure that you have all the ingredients and the time to make the dish. Sometimes recipes that I have made several times seem to vary in texture and taste – this is due to sleight of hand. In these health-conscious times, I should say that I regard all these recipes as treats, all the more enjoyable for being served on special occasions. However, you can always substitute honey for sugar, or wholemeal flour for white and so forth. We make puddings only once or twice a week for the children, and enjoy them enormously ourselves!

These are recipes that I consider to be fairly quick and simple to prepare. The ingredients for some come straight from the store cupboard (which should be well-stocked at all times) and they can therefore be knocked up in a few moments. Others are extremely expensive and are usually even quicker to make. The rules are that the best quality ingredients should be used wherever possible. Sometimes for lunch I offer only a bowl of raw vegetables and some mayonnaise. For a grander affair I might cook something simple such as asparagus. At other times I hurl several of yesterday's left-overs into ramekins or cocotte dishes, top them with grated cheese and put them under the grill. If nothing else, it is certainly a good recipe for tidying up the refrigerator.

Like many others, we often have a number of people to stay at the weekend. Although most of my friends will help me, mostly they sit about the kitchen drinking and gossiping, and that always makes me three times as slow, as I'm usually gasping with incredulity at some spicy yarn and not getting on with whatever it is I'm supposed to be doing. Therefore it is as well to have everything well prepared before Friday.

The larder before the weekend bulges and looks as though it would withstand a considerable siege for a period of months. I expect I overdo it, but then we always live on left-overs and gently recover for the rest of the week. Most of the recipes included here can be prepared in advance and re-heated when required. Everything except a soufflé will remain on hold in an Aga or hot cupboard.

Our main courses are usually game, of which there is an abundance. Game is also increasingly sold in the High Street so I have added a chapter which includes much of the game which is now available. I feel that meat and game are best if very simply cooked and served with plenty of fresh vegetables and salad. Rabbits which maraud my garden are shot from an upstairs window and gently sautéd in fresh sage and butter. Often they are turned into casseroles or added to the game pie and frozen for a later date. There are fallow and red deer, both wild and farmed, but it is the roe which is most delicious of all, and since they help themselves to my runner beans and spinach from the garden in a rather enthusiastic manner, I am learning to deal with them in a personal vendetta. However, when the deer are anywhere in the garden, we always watch them as if it is the first time we have ever seen them, as they are so beautiful. In the autumn they come very close to the house to eat the apples from the trees. If undisturbed, they will gorge themselves, eating so fast that quantities of appley froth covers their faces. Savernake was originally a medieval hunting forest for the kings of England. We have documents and seals dating back to the eleventh century, which state:

'The game within the forest to be reserved, cherished and kept for sport and pleasure of Kings and that any disturbers of the peace [poachers] sharply punished . . .'

One of the most important arrangements for a dinner party is having someone to help serve. Obviously most of us cannot afford butlers, and in our case our daily does a very good job. It adds to a very relaxed atmosphere, and it means I can talk without leaping up and down every few minutes. However, even the busiest wife with a young family can entertain in style without extra help if she plans ahead.

The first course is the most important because it sets the tone of the occasion, and the guests are not yet so engrossed in conversation that they fail to see, taste and comment upon the starter presented to them. The second course is eaten with relish but is often not thought about particularly; pudding assails your guests, rounds it all off, and then there is much settling back in chairs and . . .

One final point — a friend of mine called Jim was recently describing a meal to me and delivered this immortal line to rattle the feminist cages: 'Of course, she was *only* a cook and not a chef . . .' This set me thinking. Up until the days of petrol engines and decent roads it was often very difficult to extinguish a bad fire promptly. The remoteness of some houses, the absence of telephones and the slow speed of horse-drawn water pumps all contributed to some very terrible fires. Consequently, many fine houses, including our own in 1861, burned down. Someone once told me, or advanced the theory that in days of old some of the nobility and gentry preferred to employ chefs instead of cooks, as it was believed that voluminous and greasy skirts were highly combustible and were therefore hazardous fire-risks. Perhaps this is why cooking became a man's preserve.

There are very few famous women cooks because very few chose restaurant cooking as a career, but those who have rank as well as any of their male peers. For the rest of us, it is a sideline, a hobby or a necessity. Feeding yourself and your family is only a part of the housewife's life as a jack of all trades. Whether you are the busy wife of a banker and a career girl yourself with a dinner party to arrange and cook, or a bachelor with no kitchen maid, or a harrassed housewife like myself, who after a week with small children sees a weekend of guests with enormous appetites looming ahead, I hope this book will be of some inspiration to you.

CHAPTER 1
SOUPS

Savernake Vegetable Soup with Salami 13
Cold Mint and Pea Soup 14
Spinach Soup with Bacon 15
Celery Soup with Prawns 16
Consommé 17
Gazpacho 18
Sarah Boord's Bortsch 19

Lord Curzon was noted as having said that it was not done to serve soup at lucheon – or was it dinner? Who cares? I would rather not drink soup at a dinner party, except perhaps for a very excellent chilled soup. Hot soup seems to dull my appetite.

It goes without saying that for hot soups the tureen and bowls or plates must be hot, but many people forget that with cold soups the plates must be ice-cold. Having made the soup the day before, I put the tureen and plates into the refrigerator. It is important to remember that cold foods need more seasoning.

I occasionally thicken soups with flour or cornflour, or egg yolk and cream liaisons. However, flours seem to deaden the texture and taste, and with the liaisons there is always the danger, when in a hurry, of curdling the liquor and ending up with a sort of scrambled-egg soup. Root vegetables, when puréed, are usually thick enough. I always use more watercress than most recipes require, and pull it all together with a spoonful of mashed potato or some thick cream. Herbs should be added before puréeing or blending. Home-made stock makes a better soup than cubes and it is expedient to have a few bags of stock in the freezer, although I do use stock cubes as well, or add them to an inferior stock. Try to use the freshest ingredients whenever you have the time and inclination, and make my 'cheat' soups, such as Spinach or Mint and Pea, when you have not.

When serving the soup, reserve some of the vegetables or herbs to scatter over the top. Nearly all soups are improved aesthetically with a squiggle of cream, and always try to serve generous amounts of croûtons in bowls so that your friends can help themselves liberally.

Finally, soup made from left-overs is one of the most delicious and economical meals, and another method of tidying up the refrigerator. Put everything into the blender and add some stock and parsley. Adding some curry paste or sherry will improve a bland soup.

Savernake Vegetable Soup with Salami

Serves 4–6   Preparation time: 15 minutes   Cooking time: 30 minutes

This is a simple and easy-to-make, filling lunch-time soup. Served with hunks of bread and followed by cheese, it is one of my favourite winter lunches.

3 small potatoes
450g/1lb carrots, sliced
1 onion, sliced
Butter
Chervil
Salt and black pepper
450ml/1 pint stock
225ml/½ pint single or double
  cream
225g/½lb salami, chopped

1 Sauté the sliced vegetables in butter in a large saucepan until they are cooked. Add the chervil and season to taste.

2 Add the stock to cover the vegetables and simmer until they are tender, then mash them with a potato masher.

3 Stir in the cream, adjust the seasoning to taste and re-heat gently. Add the salami and serve hot.

Serving suggestion: Serve with croûtons (*see* page 172).

Cold Mint and Pea Soup

Serves 6   Preparation time: 10 minutes   Cooking time: 3 minutes

One summer we held a glorious gastronomic picnic in the deer park beside Burlington's Palladian summer house. We transported silver, china, food and drink and laid it on a damask-covered table beneath ancient oak trees. We sat on our dining-room chairs, waist-high in grass and wild flowers, amongst the crouching hares and browsing deer. We started with this soup which tasted all the better for its intrepid journey, having slurped dangerously close to the rim of the tureen when the driver cornered too adventurously.

450g/1lb frozen petit pois or fresh
  peas, and a handful of pods
Water
1 chicken stock cube
1 handful of mint
275ml/½ pint double or single
  cream
Seasoning

1 Reserve a handful of peas. Cover the rest of the peas with water in a pan and add the stock cube. Bring to the boil.

2 Liquidise the boiled peas with the mint. Add the seasoning and the reserved peas.

3 Adjust the consistency with more water or cream as necessary.

Serving suggestion: Chill for several hours before serving with croûtons (*see* page 172).

Spinach Soup with Bacon

Serves 4   Cooking and preparation time: 20 minutes

This is a 'cheat' soup, exceptionally quick and easy to make for when time is of the essence. It would, of course, be even more delicious made with fresh ingredients. All the ingredients are usually in everyone's larder and freezer. It takes as long as the spinach takes to melt.

225g/8oz block of frozen puréed
  spinach
295g/10.4oz tin of condensed
  chicken soup
225g/8oz bacon
150ml/¼ pint whipped double
  cream

---

1 Heat the spinach and chicken soup together.

---

2 Grill the bacon and cut it into strips.

---

3 Pour the soup into bowls with a blob of cream in the middle. Scatter bacon over the top.

Serving suggestion: Serve immediately with croûtons (*see* page 172).

Celery Soup with Prawns

Serves 8   Preparation time: 20 minutes   Cooking time: 30 minutes

The addition of prawns makes this an unusual combination.

2 heads of celery
75g/3oz butter
2 medium potatoes, sliced
1.1 litres/2 pints light chicken
*   stock*
25g/1oz butter
225g/8oz prawns

1 Chop the celery and cook it in butter in a pan until soft. Add the sliced potato and stock and simmer for 30 minutes.

2 Purée the celery mixture in a blender or pass it through a vegetable mill. Reheat it and whisk in the remaining butter.

3 Stir in the prawns and serve immediately.

Serving suggestion: Serve with croûtons (*see* page 172).

Consommé

Serves 8–10   Preparation time: 30 minutes   Cooking time: 20 minutes

I have included this recipe because it is extremely easy to make and not all that time-consuming. Laced with vodka this becomes a treat, and several flasks accompany the guns on the Savernake shoot to warm the cockles of their hearts on cold winter mornings.

2 litres/3½ pints cold stock
1.5kg/3lb shin of beef, minced or
  shredded finely
2 leeks, finely chopped
2 carrots, finely chopped
2 celery sticks, finely chopped
Handful parsley
6 egg whites, whisked in a little
  water
Salt and black pepper

1 Using a large pan, put all the ingredients into the cold stock and season well. Stir whilst the mixture warms up. Once it becomes cloudy, stop stirring.

2 Boil the mixture for at least 10 minutes until the egg has set on the surface. You will see that the liquor has cleared by gently testing with a spoon.

3 Strain the liquid through a clean tea-cloth into a bowl. Discard the meat and vegetables, which by this time are quite tasteless.

Serving suggestion: Serve hot, laced with sherry and a few added finely-chopped vegetables. If it is to be a jellied consommé, it may be necessary to add 2 leaves of gelatine, depending on the quality of your stock.

Gazpacho

Serves 8   Preparation time: 15 minutes

A lovely summer soup which is all the better for using fresh tomatoes. (Add white breadcrumbs if you use fresh tomatoes as this will slightly thicken the soup.) As speed is often important, avoid peeling and de-pipping the tomatoes by using the tinned variety if you wish. Allow extra time if you are making croûtons and dicing cucumbers, and be generous with the croûtons as everyone loves them so.

2 x 350g/14oz tins tomatoes
1 onion, roughly chopped
1 green pepper, de-seeded
2–3 cloves garlic (optional)
2 tablespoons olive oil
Juice of 1 lemon
White wine vinegar to taste
Salt and black pepper

1 Pour 1 tin of tomatoes and all the vegetables into a blender and mix until well puréed. Add the remaining tin, blend again and pass through a sieve into a large bowl.

2 Add the lemon juice and season well.

Serving suggestion: Serve chilled with the croûtons (*see* page 172) and diced cucumber served separately.

Sarah Boord's Bortsch

Makes 1.1 litres/2 pints   Preparation time: 10 minutes   Cooking time: 5 minutes

Sarah always has endless suggestions for speedy recipes – usually when I am admiring her herbaceous border and miles away from paper and pencil! But I managed to capture this one . . .

2 tins consommé
3–4 beetroot, cooked and roughly
  chopped
1 lemon, peeled with pith removed
  and chopped
Vinegar to taste
Handful of parsley, chopped

1 Pour into a food processor or blender just enough consommé to cover the beetroot and purée. The purée should be reasonably stiff, so add more consommé as necessary.

2 Mix in the remaining consommé and add the lemon and vinegar. Finally stir in the parsley.

Serving suggestion: Serve chilled with a generous swirl of sour cream to top each portion.

CHAPTER 2
HORS-D'OEUVRES

Courgette Orientale	22
Jambon Paysan de Cognac	23
Foie Gras Frais with Château d'Yquem	24
Salad and Goats' Cheese	25
Beans, Tomato, Egg and Avocado	26
Leeks Vinaigrette	27
Terrine of Vegetables with Mustard Sauce	28
Pigeon en Croûte	29
Spinach Galette with Tomato Sauce	30
Champignons à la Grecque	31
Crawlboys Pâté	32
Bernice's Caesar Salad	33
Crudités for Early Summer	34
Crudités for Winter	35
Guacamole	36
Hummus	37
Mozzarella, Avocado and Tomato Salad	38
Raw Mushrooms and Prawns with Vinaigrette	39
Mexican Salad	40
Artichoke Hearts Stuffed with Pâté	41
Raw Mushrooms with Curried Cream Sauce	42
Artichoke Heart Cream	43
Northumberland Variation	44
Salade Pitchou	45
Melon with Pinot	46
Savernake Salad	47

I love kitchen gardens. One of the most beautiful I have ever seen is the Villandry garden of Diane de Poitiers. Originally it was a formal medieval garden, probably with a mixture of herbs, aromatic and medicinal shrubs and flowers, but now it is an amazing arrangement of vegetables grown in rows, circles, and even knot shapes. Then there was the vegetable garden of a private château near Rennes. Walled and peaceful, it was seemingly filled with the glossy lines of aubergines the colour of bishops' robes, which were jostled by lettuces edged with hedges of parsley and the soldier-like leeks trying to keep them all in order. Vert de l'isle artichauts lent some glamour and elegance to a tantalising and enchanting garden. It could never become a chore to walk a quarter of a mile to that garden with a basket over one's arm, and perhaps a large straw hat to add romance and dignity to the almost ritualistic and careful selection of ingredients for the lunch-time hors-d'oeuvres. In reality, however, the gardener would discuss with the cook the requirements for the day and would return with a tray of washed vegetables. I know of a few gardens like that in England, and of one in particular in Scotland, but there it rains and the umbrella would get in the way.

Very often it is the most simple ingredients which make a delicious meal. Years ago, when I was living in Paris, I had lunch with a French friend in her kitchen. We feasted on radishes and tiny cooked brown shrimps, some of which we peeled and the smallest we crunched whole with some bread, washed down with wine. She arranged it all with such style that somehow the memory and the glorious tastes have remained with me always. I therefore recommend using the freshest, or most recently picked, ingredients for your salads. You can improve the appearance and texture of flaccid vegetables by soaking them in water. Soaking lettuces with a little sugar helps them to become more crisp. Use a salad spinner rather than dabbing at them with cloths which very often bruises them. The recipes included here should be seen merely as guides, so add or subtract according to your taste or mood, or the availability of the suggested ingredients.

As cook and hostess, it seems sensible to prepare a cold first course to be ready whenever you are. It should be able to wait for the inevitable late guests. There are a few hot dishes here and also several that are served warmed. Some of these require a little last-minute attention and it would be as well to allow for this.

Courgette Orientale

Serves 6   Preparation time: 1 hour 10 minutes   Cooking time: 10 minutes

If you increase the ingredients by half as much again this becomes an excellent main course for four people. Serve with wild rice and a green salad.

450g/1lb courgettes, sliced
Salt
Vegetable oil
Butter
4 cloves garlic, crushed
8 large tomatoes, peeled and
  quartered
225g/8oz button mushrooms, halved
2 teaspoons cumin
2 tablespoons ginger, grated
1 lemon, juice and rind
450g/1lb prawns
8 tablespoons parsley, chopped

1 Take the courgettes and salt well. Leave to stand for 1 hour. Rinse, drain and dry. Fry the courgettes in hot oil and butter in a large pan until golden but not too tender. Add the garlic and stir for 1 minute.

2 Add the tomatoes, mushrooms, spices, lemon juice and rind. Season well. Cook for a further 3–4 minutes.

3 Stir in the prawns to heat through. Finally add the parsley and pile into a hot dish.

Serving suggestion: Serve with herbed and buttered French bread.

Jambon Paysan de Cognac

Serves 6   Preparation time: 30 minutes

I first ate this recipe in the Cognac district of France. This recipe would not be as good if you used prepacked ham slices. Use only ham from the bone, or better still a hock that you have cooked yourself. It is very economical, with a slightly salty taste which balances well with the mayonnaise.

700g/2lb ham, cut into strips or
  chunks
Handful of parsley, chopped
450ml/1 pint mayonnaise (see page
  173)
Pinch saffron powder
Crushed garlic to taste
Cayenne pepper to taste

1 Arrange a generous serving of ham on each warmed serving plate. Add a layer of parsley on the top.

2 To the mayonnaise add a pinch of saffron and the crushed garlic. Pour the mayonnaise over the ham and add a sprinkle of cayenne pepper. Serve immediately.

Foie Gras Frais
with Château d'Yquem

Preparation time: 2 minutes   Cooking time: 10 minutes

This is very quick. It is also horribly expensive and will frighten the housekeeping account into oblivion, but it is luscious. I substitute Muscat French Vin de Liqueur cuvée, José Sala or similar for the Château d'Yquem if it's not available. I am not giving exact amounts because this depends on your generosity, but about 175g/6oz liver per head would be adequate.

Foie gras frais
Butter
A little endive, lightly tossed in
  vinaigrette
A few olives
Seasoning
Château d'Yquem

1 Lightly sauté the liver in butter in a large pan, and remove.

2 Arrange the endive with a few olives on each plate.

3 Season the pan juices and pour on a glass of the Yquem. Boil to reduce slightly. Pour the liquid over the livers.

Serving suggestion: Serve at once with the rest of the wine.

Salad and Goats' Cheese

Serves 4   Preparation time: 5 minutes   Cooking time: 5 minutes

A favourite salad from the Haute Savoie. The quantities suggested are a guide since it is filling. I would serve some grilled fish or chicken as a main course.

Endive, frisee lettuce or Little Gem
4 tomatoes, quartered
100g/4oz olives
Vinaigrette
4 slices bread
Butter for spreading
200g/7oz goats' cheese

1 Arrange the salad on individual plates with some olives and pour on some vinaigrette.

2 Toast the bread and lightly spread with butter, cut into 5cm/2in squares. At the same time as you are toasting the bread, warm the goats' cheese on some foil under the grill until it bubbles. Place the goats' cheese on to each of the slices of toast.

Serving suggestion: Place one slice on top of each of the salad plates. Serve immediately.

Beans, Tomato, Egg and Avocado

Serves 6   Preparation time: 20 minutes

450g/1lb French beans, lightly
  cooked and refreshed in cold
  water
6 tomatoes, peeled and sliced
2 avocados
3 eggs, hard-boiled
Mayonnaise (see page 173)
Vinaigrette (see page 174)

1 Using a large, round plate arrange the beans in a fan shape around the top edge.

2 Arrange the tomatoes in a band below these.

3 Leave a space for the avocado which must be chopped or sliced just before serving.

4 Halve the eggs, mash the yolks with a little mayonnaise, season and replace into the eggs. Arrange at the bottom of the fan.

Serving suggestion: Pour on the vinaigrette before serving.

Leeks Vinaigrette

Serves 4–6   Preparation time: 20 minutes   Cooking time: 5 minutes

It's surprising how many people love this seemingly dull starter.

1.5kg/3lb leeks
6 eggs, hard-boiled
Vinaigrette (see page 174)

1 Trim leeks to 2.5cm/1in lengths. Cook and drain well and squeeze out excess moisture on kitchen paper.

2 Separate the egg yolks from whites and chop both finely. Arrange the leeks on a platter and pour on the vinaigrette. Make a border of yellow and white egg around the edge of the platter to surround the leeks.

Terrine of Vegetables with Mustard Sauce

Serves 8   Preparation time: 30 minutes

For the terrine:
225g/8oz courgettes, halved
225g/8oz baby new carrots, halved
225g/8oz broccoli, divided into
   florets or small branches
225g/8oz French beans
12 asparagus, trimmed
2kg/4lb tomatoes, or cans of Italian
   tomatoes, puréed and sieved to
   make 1.1 litres/2 pints (add water
   if necessary)

50g/2oz gelatine, softened in a little
   hot water
Salt and pepper

For the mustard sauce:
1 tablespoon wine vinegar
2 tablespoons Dijon mustard
175g/6oz plain yoghurt
275ml/½ pint mayonnaise (see page
   173)

1 Cook all the vegetables until just tender. Refresh under cold water and dry them in kitchen paper.

2 Mix the gelatine with the tomato purée and pour into the bottom of a plastic container measuring at least 23cm/9in × 15cm/6in × 15cm/6in. Put it in the freezer for 10 minutes. Leave the remaining jelly in the fridge.

3 Arrange all the vegetables in layers on the set jelly as beautifully as possible and pour on the remaining jelly mixture. Mark the box to show the direction of layers to facilitate cutting. Leave to set in the refrigerator.

4 When set, turn out on to a plate by dipping the container in a bowl of very hot water for a few seconds.

5 To make the mustard sauce add the vinegar, mustard and yoghurt to the mayonnaise and mix well.

Serving suggestion: Cut the terrine into slices and serve with the mustard sauce. The slice from the terrine should sit in the middle of the plate surrounded by the sauce, rather like a ship at sea.

Pigeon en Croûte

Serves 4   Preparation time: 15–20 minutes   Cooking time: 15 minutes

In the autumn, our stables fill with my husband's roosting white pigeons, which, although they have their own particularly comfortable dovecote, seem to prefer the rafters above the horses. After many years of endurance I created this recipe . . .

Butter
Pigeon breasts from 2 pigeon squabs
Sage
Vinaigrette made with walnut oil
* (see page 174)*
2 raddiccio
Mâche
4 slices fried bread (kept warm)
225g/8oz walnuts and chestnuts
225g/8oz Florida condensed frozen
* orange juice*
3 tablespoons port

1 In a little butter, lightly sauté the pigeon breasts, adding a few sage leaves. Cook until they are just pink in the centres. Carve thinly and keep warm.

2 In the vinaigrette, toss the salad ingredients and arrange on individual plates. Place the fried bread in the centre of each plate. Arrange the pigeon breasts on the bread and toss the nuts into the salad.

3 Add the orange juice and port to the pan juices and boil to reduce by half. Allow to cool slightly and pour over the pigeon.

Serving suggestion: Serve immediately

Spinach Galette with Tomato Sauce

Serves 8   Preparation time: 10–15 minutes   Cooking time: 20 minutes

This rises like a soufflé but has the virtue of not sinking and can be eaten cold. In fact, we always eat it cold with cold sauce, for lunch outside in summer. The sauce is much improved if allowed to stand overnight.

450g/1lb fresh or frozen spinach
6 tablespoons double cream
4 eggs, beaten with cream
Seasoning and grated nutmeg
Tomato sauce (see page 174)

Pre-heat the oven to 200°C/400°F/Gas Mark 6.

1 Cook and drain the spinach.

2 Mix together the spinach, cream, beaten eggs and seasoning. Pour into a large loaf tin and cook in the oven at 200°C/400°F/Gas Mark 6 for 20 minutes, or until set.

3 When it is cool you can turn it out on to a plate by running a knife around the edges – this should be fairly easy to do.

Serving suggestion: Serve with the tomato sauce.

Champignons à la Grecque

Serves 8   Preparation time: 20 minutes   Cooking time: 20 minutes

Serve this with pâté as an alternative starter, although they could be eaten together.

150ml/¼ pint water or 400g/14oz
  tin crushed tomatoes
175ml/6fl oz olive oil
Juice of 3 lemons
Salt and peppercorns
Onion, chopped
Celery, to be thrown out afterwards
Herbs
1.5kg/3lb button mushrooms
2 handfuls of parsley, chopped

1 Simmer in saucepan the water or tomatoes, half the olive oil, juice of 1½ lemons, salt, peppercorns, onions, celery and herbs for 15 minutes. Pick out the peppercorns and celery and discard.

2 Throw in the button mushrooms and simmer for ten minutes. Pick out the mushrooms with a slotted spoon and put them into a bowl. Reduce the liquor to a third . Pour it over the mushrooms.

Serving suggestion: When cool, adjust the seasoning. Add masses of chopped parsley, the remaining olive oil and more lemon juice before serving.

Crawlboys Pâté

Serves 8   Cooking and preparation time: 25 minutes

Louise Guinness makes the quickest and most delicious pâté. It takes about 25 minutes. Short of sneaking into her kitchen and doing a Miss Elizabeth Mapp to her Mrs Lucas, being caught in a flash flood and floating away on her upturned kitchen table, I have with great daring asked her for the recipe and it goes like this . . .

450g/1lb chicken, duck or turkey
*   livers*
100g/4oz butter
1 dessertspoon mustard powder
Fresh thyme
2–3 cloves garlic
2 tablespoons brandy
2 tablespoons port
Bay leaves to serve

1 Sauté the meat for 5 minutes in 2oz of the butter.

2 Remove the meat, and liquidise it or crush it with a fork.

3 Return it to the pan and season with mustard powder, thyme and garlic. Pour on the brandy and simmer for 1 minute.

4 Stir in the port to taste. Put into individual pots and pour on melted butter. Set a bay-leaf on top and allow the butter to set.

Serving suggestion: Serve with thick slices of brown bread.

Bernice's Caesar Salad

Serves 4   Preparation time: 20 minutes

This is delicious before a rich main course. Bernice always puts garlic in the frying oil and anchovies in the oil for the vinaigrette.

8 tablespoons croûtons (see page
  172)
1 clove garlic
1 endive
4 tomatoes, quartered
Vinaigrette (see page 174)
Juice of ½ lemon
Worcester sauce
Anchovy essence
1 egg
175g/6oz Parmesan

1 Fry the croûtons in garlic oil, drain on kitchen paper and allow to cool. Rub 4 bowls with garlic. Arrange the endive and tomatoes in bowls.

2 Pour over the vinaigrette to which has been added the juice of half a lemon, with Worcester sauce and anchovy essence to taste. Stir in the raw beaten egg and toss the salad. Grate fresh Parmesan over the top of the salad and scatter with croûtons.

Crudités for Early Summer

Serves 4   Preparation time: 15 minutes

These are the basic ingredients for summer crudités, but it is well worth adding more exotic vegetables if they are available. Eat them with your fingers.

4–8 tiny plum tomatoes
225g/8oz button mushrooms
Head of celery, split and cut into
  finger-sized lengths
16 radishes
1 cucumber, split and cut into
  finger-sized lengths
12 young carrots
4 lettuce hearts
¼ cauliflower, broken into florets
4 bantam's eggs
225g/8oz French beans, lightly
  cooked
275ml/½ pint mayonnaise (see page
  173)
1 bunch watercress

1 Arrange the vegetables and eggs as prettily as possible on four plates.

2 Cook the watercress in 2 tablespoons of boiling water until soft and purée in a blender. Add to the mayonnaise and pour into four bowls so that the crudités may be dipped individually.

Serving suggestion: Dip the crudités into the individual bowls of green mayonnaise.

Crudités for Winter

Serves 4   Preparation time: 20 minutes

4 tomatoes, peeled and thinly sliced
225g/8oz button mushrooms, sliced
*   downwards*
1 cooked beetroot, diced
1 cucumber, peeled and sliced
100g/4oz tin of artichoke hearts
2 carrots, grated
2 hard-boiled eggs
1 celeriac, grated and mixed with
*   mayonnaise*
4 tablespoons chopped parsley
¼ cauliflower, broken into florets
225g/8oz French beans, lightly
*   cooked*
Vinaigrette (see page 174)

1 Arrange the vegetables and eggs as a flower radiating from the middle on individual plates, starting with the eggs on shredded lettuce at the centre.

2 Pour on vinaigrette just before eating.

Serving suggestion: Serve immediately.

Guacamole

Serves 8   Preparation time: 20 minutes

Guacamole and hummus (opposite) are both popular dishes but it is surprising how few people know how to make them. Easy to prepare, they could be eaten with drinks before dinner instead of a first course. Often I make both and serve them on the same plate.

4 ripe avocados, mashed with a fork
1 medium onion, grated
Juice of 1 lemon
3 cloves garlic, crushed
2 tomatoes, skinned and chopped
1 green pepper, skinned and
*   chopped*
Salt and pepper

1 Mix all the ingredients together.

2 Season well.

Serving suggestion: Serve in a glass bowl with croûtes or cold fried bread.

Hummus

Serves 6   Preparation time: 5 minutes   Cooking time: 30 minutes

450g/1lb chick peas
2–3 cloves garlic, crushed
4 tablespoons lemon juice
Pepper
Lots of mint and parsley, chopped
12 croûtes (see page 172)

1 Soak the chick peas overnight. Bring them to the boil and simmer for 30 minutes or as instructed on the packet.

2 Strain the peas of excess water if necessary and mash them with a fork. Stir in the garlic, lemon juice and ground pepper, then add the herbs.

Serving suggestion: Spread on to the cold croûtes and scatter with parsley.

Mozzarella, Avocado and Tomato Salad

Serves 6   Preparation time: 20 minutes

This recipe can be varied by adding anchovy slices, olives or capers. The best Mozzarella is sold in bags of whey and tastes much nicer than the packet varieties. It can be found in good supermarkets or Italian delicatessens.

9 ripe tomatoes
3 ripe avocados
450g/1lb Mozzarella cheese
Vinaigrette made with basil and
   garlic (see page 174)

1 Peel and slice the tomatoes and avocados.

2 Cut the Mozzarella into strips.

Serving suggestion: Arrange the salad attractively on individual plates and pour on the vinaigrette just before serving, or serve in one large salad bowl.

Raw Mushrooms
and Prawns with Vinaigrette

Serves 4   Preparation time: 10 minutes

225g/8oz button mushrooms
225g/8oz prawns
2 handfuls parsley, chopped
Vinaigrette (see page 174)

1 Chop the button mushrooms sideways.

2 Mix with the prawns and parsley.

Serving suggestion: Serve with vinaigrette poured over.

Mexican Salad

Serves 6   Preparation time: 1 hour

400g/14oz tin kidney beans
4 tablespoons vinaigrette (see page
* 174)*
1 onion, finely chopped
225g/8oz prawns
½ cucumber, cubed
1 green pepper, finely chopped
Handful chopped parsley
100g/4oz tin tuna fish
1 lemon

1 Drain the beans and mix the juice with the vinaigrette. Add the onion and marinade for 1 hour.

2 Stir the remaining ingredients together well.

Serving suggestion: Place the salad into ramekins or small indivdual bowls. Pour on the vinaigrette and serve with wedges of lemon.

Artichoke Hearts Stuffed with Pâté

Serves 4   Preparation time: 10 minutes

4 croûtes (see page 172)
225g/8oz tin artichoke hearts
100g/4oz tin of pâté (foie gras or
  smooth)
275ml/½ pint cheese sauce or
  hollandaise sauce (see page 174)

1 Make the croûtes as described on page 172.

2 Gouge out the centres of the artichoke hearts and stuff them with the pâté.

Serving suggestion: Serve the stuffed hearts on the croûtes with the sauce poured on top.

Raw Mushrooms with Curried Cream Sauce

Serves 4   Preparation time: 10 minutes

This recipe could be added to the winter crudités on page 35. I would adjust the quantities accordingly and allow several spoonfuls per person, omitting the lettuce.

500g/1lb button mushrooms
4 tablespoons mayonnaise (see page 173)
4 tablespoons soured cream
1 teaspoon curry paste
1 teaspoon tomato ketchup
Lemon juice to taste
Seasoning
Handful chives, chopped
1 lettuce, shredded

1 Slice the mushrooms in half.

2 Mix the other ingredients together and fold into the mushrooms.

Serving suggestion: Sprinkle with chives and serve on the shredded lettuce.

Artichoke Heart Cream

Serves 4   Preparation time: 15 minutes

150g/5oz soured cream
150g/5oz curd cheese
1 clove garlic, chopped
Parsley, chopped
Chives, chopped
225g/8oz tin artichoke hearts

1 Mash the cream, curd cheese, garlic, parsley and chives together.

2 Stuff the hearts and chill.

Serving suggestion: To serve, place the stuffed hearts on sprigs of lemon verbena or melissa from the herb garden.

Northumberland Variation

Serves 6   Preparation time: 25 minutes   Cooking time: 3 minutes

A friend from Northumberland used to call this her number one supper starter. She used finely chopped hard-boiled eggs, so my suggestion of scrambled eggs is the variation.

1 litre/1¾ pints jellied consommé
*   (see page 17) or 2 tins*
*   condensed consommé*
Cream to taste
8 eggs, lightly scrambled with some
*   butter*
2 green peppers, finely diced
225g/8oz smoked salmon, cut into
*   small strips*

1 Arrange the consommé, lightly forked, in a silver vegetable dish or on an oval meat platter.

2 Mix some cream with the scrambled eggs. Season well and allow to cool. Add the peppers and the smoked salmon and arrange attractively in alternate bands with the consommé.

Serving suggestion: Serve chilled.

Salade Pitchou

Serves 6   Preparation time: 15 minutes

I enjoyed this on two occasions, sitting outside a restaurant in Angoulême, Cognac. It was a very hot evening and I was already sated with too much good food. This is a very light and fresh dish, and can be followed by a rich main course.

Endive or lettuce
Vinaigrette made with walnut oil
  (see page 174)
225g/8oz walnuts
450g/1lb goats' cheese, soaked in
  walnut oil
225g/8oz black olives

1 Arrange the lettuce in individual bowls and toss well in the vinaigrette.

2 Scatter on the walnuts, black olives and the cheese, cut into bite-sized pieces.

Serving suggestion: This can be served in one large bowl but friends are always greedy with the cheese and olives!

Melon with Pinot

Serves 6   Preparation time: 10 minutes

Pinot is made from unfermented Charentais grape juice blended with old Cognac. In Cognac itself it is served ice-cold and drunk as an aperitif. It does not taste so good when brought back to England, but once in a while it makes a change from Kir and is a pleasantly unusual summer drink.

3 Ogen melons
Pinot
Raspberries to decorate

1 Cut the melons in half, scoop out the pips and pour in the Pinot to taste. I prefer to eat the melons at room temperature because chilling seems to mask their flavour.

Serving suggestion: A spoonful of raspberries in each melon half, allowed to soak in the liquids, is a pretty variation.

Savernake Salad

Serves 8   Preparation time: 30 minutes

This is a sort of 'Niçoise' with English additions.

1 crisp lettuce or endive
100g/4oz tuna
4 tomatoes, quartered
450g/1lb Jersey potatoes mixed
  with mayonnaise
450g/1lb French beans, boiled for 5
  minutes
4 hard-boiled eggs, quartered
225g/8oz prawns
30 black olives
50g/2oz anchovy fillets
1 handful chives, chopped
1 handful parsley, chopped
Vinaigrette (see page 174)

1 A few moments before eating, toss the lettuce in vinaigrette and arrange in individual bowls with the potatoes in the middle.

2 Arrange the rest of the ingredients around the potatoes in the dish.

Serving suggestion: Scatter the herbs and pour on some more vinaigrette.

CHAPTER 3

PASTA

Louise's Carbonara	49
Annie Bruce's Pasta	50
Pasta and Soft Blue Cheese	51
Pasta with Cream, Ham and Mushrooms	52
Mary's Fettucine Alfredo	53

How I adore Italian food! These recipes are the plundered and Anglicised versions I have collected, so perhaps this section should really be called 'Imperfect Pasta'.

Fresh spaghetti and pasta in various shapes is available from all good delicatessens and excellent brands can now be obtained from many supermarkets. Now that fresh pasta is readily available I prefer not to use the dried variety.

Drop a little olive oil into the boiling salted water before adding the pasta as this helps to prevent the strands from sticking together. As soon as it is cooked (3 minutes or so to al dente) drain and add a little more heated oil for a slightly glossy appearance. Again, this helps to keep it all separate. Allow about 50g/2oz pasta per person for a first course and follow with grilled fish, chicken or a light game dish.

We often eat pasta for supper, consuming horrifying amounts served with green salad and drinking some Soave or Vinho Verde. Sometimes I make pesto sauce or a simple tomato and onion sauce with lots of basil and black pepper. The next day, if any is left over, I mix all the ingredients together with some chopped meat or bacon, add some butter and place it all into an ovenproof dish in an extremely hot oven so that the top and sides become golden and crisp. This might make enough for one person's lunch or to accompany a main course as a substitute for potatoes.

Louise's Carbonara

Serves 4   Preparation time: 5 minutes   Cooking time: 10 minutes

We eat quantities of this with green salad and I would make it as a starter if we were eating in the kitchen. It must be eaten as soon as it is ready.

450g/1lb bacon rashers
250g/10oz pasta
2 tablespoons olive oil, heated
4 eggs, beaten
Freshly ground black pepper
Parmesan, grated

1 Grill or fry the bacon and cut into strips. Keep hot.

2 Put the pasta in boiling, salted water and cook for about 3 minutes. Drain.

3 Pour the heated oil and bacon fat over the pasta, quickly followed by the eggs, Stir well so that the eggs coat and are cooked on the hot pasta. Season well with lots of freshly ground black pepper.

4 Add the bacon and serve immediately.

Serving suggestion: Serve the Parmesan separately, to be sprinkled on top.

Annie Bruce's Pasta

Serves 8   Preparation time: 15 minutes   Cooking time: 10 minutes

Do not overcook the prawns or they will become hard and tasteless.

450g/1lb small shell pasta
575ml/1 pint double cream
100g/4oz fresh Parmesan, grated
450g/1lb prawns
3 thick slices smoked salmon,
  chopped roughly
Pepper

1 Boil the pasta in salted water until cooked. Drain and keep hot.

2 Melt the cream and cheese together and season well. Gently warm the prawns in this sauce and pour over the cooked pasta shells, mixing well. Scatter the salmon on top.

Serving suggestion: Serve immediately.

Pasta and Soft Blue Cheese

Serves 4   Preparation time: 25 minutes   Cooking time: 10 minutes

This delicious pasta recipe is based on dishes sampled in Rome during a memorable holiday.

225g/8oz fresh pasta
1 tablespoon olive oil
150g/5oz Gorgonzola, Roquefort or
  Dorset Blue cheese
50g/2oz butter
Milk
275ml/½ pint double cream
Freshly grated Parmesan

1 Cook the pasta in boiling salted water and toss in a little olive oil to prevent it sticking.

2 Mash the cheese with the butter and milk. Heat the cream and pour on to the cheese mixture. Thoroughly mix in with the pasta.

Serving suggestion: Serve with grated Parmesan.

Pasta with Cream, Ham and Mushrooms

Serves 4   Preparation time: 20 minutes   Cooking time: 20 minutes

Another favourite from Italy.

1 medium onion, finely chopped
125g/5oz butter
225g/8oz button mushrooms, finely
*   chopped*
150g/5oz ham or grilled bacon
275ml/½ pint double cream
375g/12oz pasta
Freshly grated Parmesan

1 Sauté the onion in 1oz butter until soft and golden. Add and cook the mushrooms and season. Toss in the ham and half the cream and keep warm.

2 Cook the pasta in boiling salted water for 3 minutes. Drain and keep hot.

3 Melt the remaining butter and cream in another pan and pour over the drained pasta, stirring in the cheese.

4 Make a dent in each serving and put the mushroom mixture in the middle.

Serving suggestion: Serve with extra Parmesan.

Mary's Fettucine Alfredo

Makes 6   Preparation time: 15 minutes   Cooking time: 5 minutes

225g/8oz bacon, ham or veal
125g/5oz butter
250g/9oz Barilla tagliatelle or fresh
  pasta
575ml/1 pint single cream
8 tablespoons fresh grated
  Parmesan
Salt and pepper
Seasoning and nutmeg

1 Fry the bacon, ham or veal in 1oz butter and chop into small pieces when cooked. Keep hot.

2 Cook the pasta in boiling salted water for 3 minutes. Drain and keep hot.

3 Melt the remaining butter in a pan, stir in the cream and cheese and simmer until the sauce is smooth. Season. Combine the sauce with the pasta. Cover the pan with a lid and allow to stand in a warm place for 2 minutes.

4 Scatter the chopped meat over the pasta and sauce.

CHAPTER 4
EGGS

Exotic Eggs in Little Pots	56
My Eggs Benedict	57
A Good Egg	58
Eggs in Blue Cheese	59
Eggs and Eel on a Croûte	60
Creamed Eggs with Black Lumpfish Roe	61

The inestimable, esteemed egg is an invaluable ingredient for many dishes. There are so many uses for eggs that it is right we think favourably of them. There they are, arranged in their earthenware bowl, ready to suffer grievous bodily harm for the cause of haute cuisine! They are whisked into soufflès, beaten senseless for scrambled eggs, poached in boiling water and their yolks have olive oil forced into them to make mayonnaise. The list of their sufferings is endless. My favourite egg is oeuf à la coque and soldiers. Thinly sliced fingers of buttered toast dipped into runny yolks, this has no peer and is something my husband can do a great deal better than I, since the telephone or some other interruption always causes me to forget the length of time the eggs have been boiling.

One evening we were having supper with friends and it was suggested that if an egg is thrown into the air it will land on its end and, due to weight distribution, will not break. We decided to test the theory and started tossing eggs about in the kitchen. This was unpopular with the mistress of the house, and after several broken eggs we decided that the lack of height could be the cause of the failure. So we repaired outside with a dozen eggs or so. Imagine the scene – a summer's evening, a low stone-roofed Cotswold house, a group on one side and a man on the other with a golfing umbrella. The scientific experiment was carefully monitored with each of us throwing an egg over the roof and the success and failure rate being duly shouted back. Almost all the eggs broke but our host's three dogs had a delicious breakfast on the lawn the next morning.

Here are a few ideas to try for yourself (all except the plover or lapwings):

Quail – Fresh, hard-boiled and piled up in a bowl, quail's eggs, with their pretty shells, make an extremely attractive appetiser with drinks before dinner. Arrange a few plates strategically piled with generous amounts of celery salt. Your guests can crack and discard the shells and dip into the salt and some people consider they are most delicious eaten whole, shell and all!

Pheasant — These can be obtained if you know someone who rears pheasants for shooting, either infertile eggs which therefore will not hatch, or eggs surplus to requirements. Serve as for quail eggs. Sometimes I make pheasant egg mousse which is very rich and a beautiful deep yellow. On other occasions I halve and hard-boil the eggs and mix the yolks with mayonnaise. The mixture is then spooned back into the cavity. Scatter on some parsley and these make an excellent appetiser, or they can be added to a plate of crûdités.

Green plover, lapwing or peewit — These used to be plentiful and as the hen lays several eggs (to allow for natural predators) it was always considered permissible to take just one from each nest on the ground. Nowadays, due to rollers and the use of agricultural chemicals, these birds are scarce and so protected.

Bantam — If all the other types of egg are unavailable or too expensive, these are a very acceptable substitute. Try decorating the shells with dark green food dyes; a spattering of dark green and brown may fool quite a few people.

Exotic Eggs in Little Pots

Makes 6   Preparation time: 20 minutes   Cooking time: 5 minutes

Another simple supper dish for two, or a reasonably rich starter for six. This recipe can be found in many cookery books with varying ingredients and always with an exotic-sounding title.

6 hard-boiled eggs, chopped
225g/8oz prawns
1 small jar Dijon mustard
275ml/½ pint double cream
Handful of parsley, chopped
175g/6oz grated Gruyère

1 Mix all the ingredients except the cheese together and place in small, ovenproof pots or dishes.

2 Sprinkle with cheese and grill until golden.

Serving suggestion: Serve immediately.

My Eggs Benedict

Serves 4   Preparation time: 15 minutes   Cooking time: 5 minutes

Another classical French recipe much simplified and very delicious.

4 crumpets
50g/2oz butter
2 large slices ham
4 eggs
275ml/½ pint double cream
Salt and pepper
2 teaspoons English mustard
100g/4oz strong Cheddar cheese,
*   finely grated*

1 Toast the crumpets and cut them into four squares. Spread with butter immediately and keep warm on a suitable serving dish.

2 Shape the ham to match the crumpets allowing the edges to flop over the sides of the crumpets.

3 Poach the eggs in an egg poacher. Meanwhile season the cream with salt, pepper and mustard and boil for 2 minutes so that it thickens. Stir in the cheese and remove from the heat – the cheese will melt in the hot cream.

4 Put the ham on to the crumpet and then the egg, pour on the cream and dust the tops with cayenne. Serve immediately.

A Good Egg

Serves 4   Preparation time: 15 minutes   Cooking time: 5 minutes

An excellent starter before some roasted meat, or a delicious and simple supper dish for two followed by salad, fruit and cheese.

1 finely chopped onion
25g/1oz butter
150ml/¼ pint double cream
Anchovy essence
Salt and pepper
4 eggs

Pre-heat the oven to 200°C/400°F/Gas Mark 6.

1 Fry the onion in the butter until soft. Stir in the cream and anchovy essence to taste and season.

2 Pour half the mixture into ramekins. Break eggs on to the onion mixture and cover with remainder of the mixture. Bake in the oven at 200°C/400°F/Gas Mark 6 or until egg is cooked.

Serving suggestion: Serve at once.

Eggs in Blue Cheese

Serves 4   Preparation time: 10 minutes   Cooking time: 5 minutes

A fairly substantial start to a meal, this also makes a simple dish for supper for two. I always use individual dishes.

25g/1oz butter
4 eggs
4 heaped tablespoons any blue
*   cheese*
150ml/¼ pint single cream,
*   seasoned with salt and pepper*
4 rashers of bacon, fried and
*   chopped*

Pre-heat oven to 200°C/400°F/Gas Mark 6.

1 Put the ramekins into the oven with knobs of butter at 200°C/400°F/Gas Mark 6 to melt the butter. Remove from the oven.

2 Break the eggs into the ramekins and scatter half the bacon on top. Add cheese and cream.

3 Bake for five minutes in the oven or until the egg-white has set – test with a finger.

4 Scatter the rest of the bacon on top.

Serving suggestion: Serve immediately.

Eggs and Eel on a Croûte

Serves 4   Preparation and cooking time: 15 minutes

This excellent dish also makes a very good savoury but the egg must be eaten immediately and goes rubbery if kept warm for too long.

25g/1oz butter
4 eggs
150ml/¼ pint single cream
Salt and pepper
225g/½lb smoked eel
4 croûtes (see page 172)

1 Make very creamy scrambled egg by melting the butter in the top of a double boiler and stirring the eggs frequently until set. Stir in the cream and season.

2 Place strips of extremely thinly sliced eel on the croûtes, spoon the egg over the eel and then place more eel on the top.

Serving suggestion: Serve at once.

Creamed Eggs
with Black Lumpfish Roe

Makes 6   Cooking time: 20 minutes   Preparation time: 20 minutes

I made this for a Glyndebourne picnic arranged in Victorian silver egg holders bedded on lots of lemon verbena.

6 large fresh eggs
25g/1oz butter
1 tablespoon finely chopped onion
2 teaspoons finely scissored chives
3 tablespoons cream
Seasoning
75g/3oz black lumpfish roe

1 Either saw off the top of the eggs with a serrated knife or chip them off.

2 Beat the eggs and strain them into a double boiler with the butter. Stir until creamy – *do not* overcook. Stir in onion and chives, cream and seasoning.

3 Pour back into the shells.

Serving suggestion: Serve in egg-cups topped with the lumpfish roe.

CHAPTER 5
FISH

Celeriac Rémoulade with Mussels	64
A Little Plate of Seafood	65
Salmon rolled around Prawns	66
Turbot and Bacon in a Creamy Sauce with a Hat	67
Lobster with Sauce Maltaise	68
Baked Stuffed Mussels	69
Prawn and Cucumber Mousse	70
Lobster Creams	71
Torridon Mussels	72
Brian's Beluga and Salmon	73
Gravadlax and Dill Sauce	74
Jobiska's Fish	75
Skewered Seafood	76
Terrine of Salmon	77
Filet de Sole Montmorency	78
Russian Haddock	79
Sea Trout	80
Prawns in Savoury Green Mousse	81

'Only the best is ever the best,' said Madame Prunier. She meant it of all recipe ingredients, but it is never more true than with fish. The famous fish restauranteur took a very close interest in the Tante Marie School and was a friend of the founder. At the end of the year she presented the diplomas. Consequently we were taught 'fish', and it became a speciality of the school. Perhaps because my star sign is Pisces, I like looking at fish, although I am not too fond of shellfish and I dislike trout.

One of the best and simplest ways of cooking salmon and sea trout is to wrap them in foil with some fennel, butter and lemon slices, seasoned with freshly ground black pepper. The most romantic method is that used by the smuggler for his mistress in Daphne du Maurier's book *Frenchman's Creek*. This is a sort of piratical grill you can adapt by pre-heating your grill, and stuffing the insides and covering the outsides of the fish with fresh herbs such as dill or fennel. Let the fish skin and the herbs blister and burn. The flesh will be succulent and subtle in flavour.

Whenever I am in London I always try to visit the food halls of Harrods. The fish are a particular delight, and the different varieties of seafood and shellfish encourage new ideas. A grand salad of shredded lettuce mixed with some clams, mussels, prawns and smoked oysters in a light dressing of vinaigrette, served with a wedge of lemon makes a fish dish fit for a king. Make it even grander with some monkfish tail, a coulis of tomato, some avocado and artichoke fonds and it is thoroughly *nouvelle cuisine*. Neither of these ideas take much time since all the ingredients are bought ready-cooked or are eaten raw. They would also make an excellent first course.

I know of a man who advised his first wife, as a new bride, that she was never on any account to cook or serve him fish. If she did so he would divorce her. Several years later, having quite forgotten his warning (or had she?), she did and he did! The following recipes are for those of you who have received no such warning.

Celeriac Rémoulade with Mussels

Serves 4   Preparation time: 1 hour   Cooking time: 25 minutes

1 celeriac root, finely grated
2 teaspons salt
2 teaspoons lemon juice
40 mussels, cleaned and scraped
275ml/¹/₂ pint mayonnaise (see page
   173)
3 tablespoons Dijon mustard
4 tablespoons parsley, chopped

1 Steep the celeriac in cold water, salt and lemon juice for 1 hour.

2 Steam the mussels in their wet shells in a large frying pan until they are open. Remove the mussels from their shells and discard the shells.

3 Place the mayonnaise in a large bowl and whisk in the mustard.

4 Drain and dry the celeriac. Mix it into the mayonnaise. Add the mussels, reserving a few to decorate the finished dish. Lastly stir in the parsley.

Serving suggestion: Decorate with a few mussels before serving.

A Little Plate of Seafood

Serves 6   Preparation time: 10 minutes   Cooking time: 30 minutes

450g/1lb cod steaks
8 scallops
4 Dublin Bay prawns
16 mussels, washed and scraped
8 large mushrooms, chopped
4 baby courgettes, chopped
275ml/½ pint hollandaise sauce
  (see page 174)
50g/2oz grated cheese

1 Steam the fish between 2 ovenproof plates over a pan of hot water.

2 Steam the vegetables in a colander over hot water until lightly cooked.

3   Arrange the fish and vegetables in a buttered, oval ovenproof dish. Pour on the sauce and scatter with grated cheese. Grill until browned.

Serving suggestion: Serve immediately.

Salmon rolled around Prawns

Makes 4   Preparation time: 15 minutes

This is extremely rich and very extravagant. It must be followed by a simple main course such as a roast lamb with a green salad.

2 tablespoons tomato purée
6 tablespoons mayonnaise (see page
  173)
8oz prawns, peeled
Black pepper
4 large slices smoked salmon or
  enough to make 8 lengths of
  approximately 7.5cm/3in x
  15cm/6in
Cayenne pepper
1 bunch watercress
2 lemons

1 Mix the tomato purée with the mayonnaise and season with freshly ground black pepper. Stir in the prawns.

2 Place the mixture on the middle of each piece of salmon and roll up. Dust the tops with cayenne.

Serving suggestion: Place the rolls on a bed of watercress and surround with thick lemon wedges. Serve with thinly sliced bread and butter.

Turbot and Bacon
in a Creamy Sauce with a Hat

Serves 8   Cooking and preparation time: 30 minutes

This is an adaptation from a delightful book of nursery food by Jane Torday. Nearly all of her recipes make delicious grown-up eating. It is a particular favourite of mine and our friends. Any white and close-fleshed fish will do. For the 'hat' we are fortunate to be able to buy fresh, uncooked pastry from a local baker. However, I recommend Saxby's if you do not have an enlightened baker near you.

For the fish:
675g/1½lb white fish
575ml/1 pint milk
50g/2oz butter
3 bay-leaves
Seasoning
Parsley
450g/1lb bacon, cut into cubes and
  fried

For the sauce:
100g/4oz butter
2 tablespoons plain flour
1 generous glass white wine
150ml/¼ pint double cream

For the hats:
450g/1lb puff pastry
1 egg, beaten

Pre-heat the oven to 200°C/400°F/Gas Mark 6.

---

1 Poach the fish in a large pan with the milk, butter, bay-leaves, seasoning and parsley until cooked. Flake the fish into large chunks.

---

2 Make the sauce by combining the butter, flour and wine. Boil for 3 minutes and then add the cream.

---

3 To make the hats, roll the puff pastry out and cut it into crescents. Brush with egg and bake until golden at approximately 200°C/400°F/Gas Mark 6.

---

4 Combine the fish mixture with the sauce and then add the bacon. Decorate the fish mixture with the hats and a scattering of parsley. Serve in an oval fish dish.

Lobster with Sauce Maltaise

Serves 8   Preparation time: 30 minutes

For the lobster:
3 Little Gem lettuces or radiccio
1.5kg/3lb lobster, cooked and split
2 oranges, divided into segments
  without membraneous skin

For the sauce:
2 quantities hollandaise sauce (see
  page 174)
1 orange, squeezed and grated

1 Tear the lettuce finely and put on to eight plates. Shred the lobster and place it on top.

2 Crack the lobster claws, remove the meat and slice it length-wise. Arrange the meat alternately with the orange segments on the plates.

3 To make the sauce maltaise, put the hollandaise in a bowl and mix in the squeezed and grated orange. Pour over the shredded lobster.

Serving suggestion: This can be left on the table until you are ready to eat it – beware of the cat!

Baked Stuffed Mussels

Serves 4   Preparation time: 1 hour   Cooking time: 5 minutes

Although this recipe takes some time to prepare it is always greeted with great appreciation and is scrumptious. Allow 12 mussels per head. It is a good idea to make a bowl of crudités and some mayonnaise as well, since there is always someone who will be allergic to shellfish. The others will have no trouble eating a few more.

48 mussels, washed and scraped
1 onion
1 clove garlic
225g/8oz butter
6 tablespoons breadcrumbs
6 tablespoons parsley, chopped
Salt and pepper

Pre-heat the oven to 200°C/400°F/Gas Mark 6.

1 Cook the mussels in a shallow pan in their own steam. Remove as soon as they open. Loosen the mussels from their shells, replace them and put them on a baking sheet.

2 Sweat the onion and garlic in the butter until soft and transparent. Stir in the breadcrumbs and parsley and season. Spoon this mixture over the fish in their shells.

3 Bake in a hot oven (200°C/400°F/Gas Mark 6) until golden.

Serving suggestion: Arrange the mussels on a large platter. Keep warm and serve within 15 minutes.

Prawn and Cucumber Mousse

Serves 8   Preparation time: 30 minutes   Marinade: 1 hour

1 cucumber, peeled and finely diced
3 teaspoons salt
6 tablespoons white wine vinegar
450g/1lb cream cheese
150ml/¼ pint double cream
225ml/8fl oz mayonnaise (see page
*   173)*
25g/1oz gelatine, softened in a little
*   hot water*
350g/12oz prawns, peeled
1 teaspoon each of paprika and
*   cayenne pepper*
8 tablespoons chives, chopped
2 lemons and bread to serve

---

1 Soak the cucumber in salt and vinegar for 30 minutes, drain in a sieve and leave for a further 30 minutes. Dry with kitchen paper.

---

2 Beat the cheese until creamy and stir in the cream and mayonnaise. Season with the paprika and pepper and add the chives. Stir in the gelatine.

---

3 Stir in the prawns and cucumber. Spoon into a 25cm/10in soufflé dish, or similar, and chill.

Serving suggestion: Serve with wedges of lemon and toast.

Lobster Creams

Serves 6   Preparation time: 30 minutes   Cooking time: 10 minutes

This recipe came from *Annie's Edwardian Cookery Book* compiled by Joan Haine, who befriended Annie while she was cooking for a local village school. What lucky children they must have been! Annie had been an assistant cook in service at Tottenham House, Wiltshire, to my husband's great-grandfather. I would make this as a pâté brisé and press it into barquettes, or boat-shaped tins, but a slightly simpler method is given here.

450g/1lb short pastry
275ml/½ pint double cream,
   whipped
Pepper, salt and cayenne
700g/2lb lobster meat, cooked and
   shredded
Red lumpfish roe (optional)

Pre-heat the oven to 200°C/400°F/Gas Mark 6.

---

1 Roll out the pastry, cut individual pieces and shape them into a jam-tart tray. Bake blind (*see* below) in an oven at 200°C/400°F/Gas Mark 6 until golden (about 5 minutes). Turn out and allow to cool on a wire rack.

---

2 Season the cream with lots of freshly ground pepper, salt and cayenne. Mix with the lobster meat and fill the pastry cases.

Serving suggestion: Decorate with some of the coral or use some red lumpfish roe.

Note: To bake blind, line a pie dish or tin with pastry and prick the base with a fork. Line with bakewell paper and weight with rice. When the pastry is cooked, remove from the oven, take out the paper and rice and return to the oven for one minute to dry the base. I keep rice in a jar and have re-used the same rice for years.

Torridon Mussels

Serves 4   Preparation time: 30 minutes   Cooking time: 5 minutes

We picked the mussels for this ourselves on the edge of Upper Loch Torridon, a sea loch, and the recipe was given to us by the postmaster, Donny. The tin of milk does sound rather dubious but this recipe is delicious.

1 onion, chopped
25g/1oz butter
2 litres/3½ pints mussels, scraped
    and cleaned
150ml/4oz tin evaporated milk

1 Fry or sauté the onion in a large, flat pan until soft and transparent.

2 Put the mussels into the pan to steam in their wet shells. When they open, remove on to large soup plates.

3 There will be a lot of juice in the pan by now. Add the tin of milk and heat it up. Pour over the mussels before serving.

Serving suggestion: Serve straight from the pan.

Brian's Beluga and Salmon

Serves 2   Preparation time: 20 minutes

Brian is a friend and bon viveur who sometimes does the washing-up after dinner at his home and rewards himself with a half-bottle of champagne.

2 hard-boiled eggs
2 tablespoons mayonnaise (see page
 173)
225g/8oz smoked salmon
1 Little Gem lettuce
8 Dublin Bay prawns, peeled
2 tablespoons beluga (optional)
2 tablespoons red lumpfish roe
2 tablespoons black lumpfish roe
Buttered brown bread
Lemon wedges

1 Halve the eggs. Take out the yolks and mix with mayonnaise. Season and put them back into the cavities.

2 Curl the salmon into the contours of the lettuce and arrange on a plate with the eggs.

3 Arrange the remaining ingredients in heaps.

Serving suggestion: Hand round the bread and lemon wedges on a separate plate.

Gravadlax and Dill Sauce

Serves 6   Preparation time: 30 minutes   Marinade: 4 days

Another recipe from a friend of mine, Jan, who is one of the best, most inventive cooks I know.

For the marinade
2kg/4lb trout or salmon, boned and
  filleted
1 tablespoon sea salt
1 tablespoon brown sugar
5 tablespoons dill, chopped
3 tablespoons brandy or sherry

For the sauce:
4 tablespoons dark French mustard
3 tablespoons runny honey or caster
  sugar
2 tablespoons white wine vinegar or
  tarragon
3 tablespoons corn oil
1 tablespoon powdered mustard
3 tablespoons chopped dill
Crushed garlic (optional)

1 Check the fillets for small bones and remove them.

2 Rub all sides of the fish with the marinade mixture, wrap in clingfilm, cover with foil and put in a plastic container under heavy weights for 4 days. After 2 days unwrap and spoon marinade over the fish again. Rewrap as before.

3 Make the dill sauce by putting all the ingredients into a blender or hand whisking as for mayonnaise. This sauce keeps for several weeks in the refrigerator.

4 Put the fish in the freezer for several hours to make carving easier. Slice the fish thinly and arrange on plates decorated with dill.

Serving suggestion: Serve the sauce separately with brown bread and butter.

Jobiska's Fish

Serves 4   Preparation time: 10 minutes   Cooking time: 17 minutes

My interest in food was sharpened when as a child I read the poem *The Pobble who has no toes*. His Aunt Jobiska:

> ' . . made him a feast at his earnest wish
> of eggs and buttercups fried with fish;
> And she said, "It's a fact the whole world knows,
> That Pobbles are happier without their toes."'

This seemed to me to be epicurean delight. If you are feeling at all eccentric, which I frequently do, you could scatter a few buttercups about the dish.

450g/1lb smoked haddock, filleted
Butter
3 tomatoes, peeled and sliced
275ml/½ pint double cream,
* seasoned*
50g/2oz butter
4 eggs
Triangles of toast or fried bread to
* serve*

Pre-heat the oven to 180°C/350°F/Gas Mark 4

---

1 Slice the fillets up the middle and place in an oval sole dish which has been well buttered. Add a layer of tomatoes and seasoned cream. Blob with butter and cook in the oven at 180°C/350°F/Gas Mark 4 for about 12 to 15 minutes until the fish is nearly done.

---

2 Remove from the oven and break the eggs on to the fish and tomatoes and spoon some of the cream over the tops of the eggs. Cook in the oven for a further 5 minutes.

Serving suggestion: Serve with triangles of toast or fried bread.

Skewered Seafood

Serves 4   Preparation time: 10 minutes   Cooking time: 5 minutes   Marinade
time: 1 hour

For the marinade:
3 tablespoons olive oil
3 tablespoons dry sherry
1 teaspoon granulated sugar
2 cloves garlic
1 teaspoon salt
Ground pepper
4 shallots or 1 onion, chopped

For the fish:
16 scallops
16 Dublin Bay prawns
Stoned black olives
*275g/½ pint mayonnaise (see page
   173)*
1 lemon

---

1 Marinade the fish for 1 hour or longer.

---

2 Skewer the fish and olives and grill until cooked. Brush on the marinade
   while cooking.

Serving suggestion: Serve with mayonnaise and lemon wedges.

Terrine of Salmon

Serves 8   Preparation time: 30 minutes   Marinade: 1 hour   Chilling time: Overnight

Pretty to look at, delicious to eat and terribly easy to make. Do not be daunted by that, because your guests will be very impressed.

700g/2lb salmon off the bone
White wine
5 tablespoons chopped parsley
2 tablespoons chopped tarragon and
  chervil
10 teaspoons green peppercorns
5 shallots, finely chopped
50g/2oz gelatine, softened in a little
  hot water
3 400g/14oz tins of tomatoes,
  puréed and strained

Juice of 2 lemons
1 tin red pimento
8 lemons or limes peeled without
  pith and roughly chopped
5 hard-boiled eggs, separated and
  roughly chopped
Lemon verbena or mint leaves to
  garnish

1   Marinade the salmon for 1 hour in the wine and herbs, 8 teaspoons peppercorns and finely chopped shallots. Reserve 2 teaspoons for the layering.

2   Leave the fish in the marinade to cool. Drain.

3   Stir the dissolved gelatine into the tomato purée and add the lemon juice. Pour a little of the jelly mixture into the terrine and allow to set. Keep the remaining jelly at the consistency of custard.

4   Make alternate layers of jelly, salmon and the remaining ingredients, with the layers of salmon running lengthways and finish with the jelly. Put the terrine into the fridge to set completely.

5   To turn out, dip the terrine into a bowl of boiling water for a few seconds and loosen the edges with a knife. Put a plate on the top of the terrine and invert it. Leave in a fridge or cold place overnight. Cut into slices and put on plates.

Serving suggestion: Decorate with lemon verbena or improvise if you have none. Serve with a tomato mayonnaise (see page 173).

Note: A large, empty plastic ice-cream box would make an excellent mould for this recipe.

Filet de Sole Montmorency

Serves 4   Preparation and cooking time: 30 minutes

This is a grand, classical French dish, somewhat simplified. It will keep hot in the warming oven if well-covered with a lid and greaseproof paper.

8 sole fillets
1 glass white wine
1 glass water
Herbs and parsley
25g/1oz butter
75g/3oz button mushrooms
15g/½oz plain flour
150ml/¼ pint double cream
Salt and pepper
100g/4oz prawns
8 crescent shapes of puff pastry
  (fleurons)

1 Poach the fish in the wine, water and herbs. Remove and keep hot.

2 Soften the mushrooms in a little butter. When they are soft, stir in the flour, pour on the fish liquor and thicken.

3 Add the cream and seasoning, then add the prawns.

4 Cook the pastry crescents separately in a very hot oven, in the last 3 minutes before serving. Arrange the fish on individual plates and pour on sauce.

Serving suggestion: Serve hot with the pastry fleurons.

Russian Haddock

Serves 4   Preparation time: 5 minutes   Freezing time: 30 minutes

This was originally made by a rather enterprising man for a dinner party and is delicious. Needless to say we all became completely legless. I think we had steak next but no one can remember.

450g/1lb smoked haddock fillets
3 eggs, beaten
Juice of 2 lemons
Pepper
Vodka, iced, to serve
Bread for toast, to serve

1 Mash up the raw haddock with the beaten eggs.
Squeeze the lemons and add to the mixture, seasoning well.

2 Put the mixture in the freezer for half an hour, then leave it in the fridge for several hours.

Serving suggestion: Serve *very cold* with toast and iced vodka.

Sea Trout

Serves 4   Preparation time: 5 minutes   Cooking time: 30 minutes

My favourite dish and the only trout for me. In season, from spring to midsummer, sea trout are best at about the same time as early broad beans, which I would serve with the trout, if it was to be a main course.

900g/2½lb sea trout
Salt and black pepper
100g/4oz butter
Juice of 1 lemon
Fresh tarragon (optional)
Hollandaise sauce (see page 174)
Lemon wedges

Pre-heat the oven to 180°C/350°F/Gas Mark 4.

1 Lay the fish on two large strips of foil. Season well. Add a few blobs of butter inside and outside the fish, and pour on the lemon juice. Sprinkle with fresh tarragon if liked.

2 Wrap up the fish like a gondola, with the ends curved upwards to ensure that no juice can escape. Bake at 180°C/350°F/Gas Mark 4 for 30 minutes.

Serving suggestion: Place the foil gondolas on to a serving plate and unwrap just before serving at the table. Serve with hollandaise sauce and lemon wedges.

Prawns in Savoury Green Mousse

Serves 6   Preparation and cooking time: 40 minutes

This dish is very light and may be followed by a fairly rich main course, although I think it is most agreeable not to have a rich menu.

Salt
1 cucumber, finely sliced
275ml/½ pint double cream
25g/1oz gelatine, melted in a little
    hot water
225g/8oz prawns
Seasoning to taste
3 egg-whites
Paprika
1 lemon

1 Sprinkle salt over the cucumber slices. After 1 hour blot away excess moisture with kitchen paper and liquidise.

2 Whisk the cream to a custard consistency, stir in the gelatine and add the prawns and puréed cucumber. Season and chill.

3 When the mixture is on the point of setting, fold in the stiffly whisked egg-whites. Pour into glass bowls and dust the tops with paprika. Allow to set.

Serving suggestion: Serve with lemon wedges.

CHAPTER 6
GAME

Pheasant on Watercress	85
Pheasant à la Normande	86
Chinese Pheasant	87
Woodcock	88
Partridge with Tarragon	89
Haunch of Roe	90
Redcurrant Pot of Venison	91
Roast Saddle of Hare in Brandy and Cream	92
Saddle of Fallow in Orange Sauce	93
Pigeon and Rabbit Terrine	94
Savernake Pigeon Pie	95

Here are a few recipes and suggestions for cooking the game which is easily available to us in Savernake Forest – deer, rabbit, hare, squirrel, pheasant, partridge, pigeon, rook, woodcock and collared doves. Even hedgehogs are considered by some to be excellent and the gypsies used to cover them with clay and bake them in the embers of the fire, so that when broken the spines came away with the hardened clay. As far as other possiblities go, my small son has mentioned sightings, imaginary or otherwise, of bears and dragons. The ancient hunting horn of the family shows drawings of strange animals and birds which may have been hunted, but the strangest of all is a unicorn. We also have a record of a wonderful feast held in the forest for King Henry VIII (for it was in Savernake that he was to meet the only one of his wives to give him a son – King Edward VI – namely Jane Seymour who was a distant ancestor of my husband.) For one Sunday lunch they ate 6 oxen, 24 sheep, 21 great, 7 good, 11 Kentish and 42 coarse capon, and also:

'Pullets, chickeyns, veales, 5 cygnets. 7 swans, 2 cranes, 2 storks, 3 pheasant and 40 partridge. Quails, mewes, egretts, pea chicks, synts [snipe], 2-dozen lark, 6 brewes and 28 gulls.'

There were many guests with retinues of servants and on the King's tables alone 470 portions were served. This was all washed down with 'swete and Gascon wine, bere, aill' and a spiced wine known as hippocras. What a party!

Although my family eat very little meat, we do occasionally eat game.

One of my favourite ideas is to serve a plain roast meat with a salad of chicory or lamb's lettuce, with a wedge of Dorset cheese to clear the palate. Mostly I prefer game to be roasted and it should be hung long enough to tenderise but not so long that it becomes putrefied. Venison should be eaten within 3 or 4 days as too long hanging dries out the meat. The meats, having been simply roasted, are best accompanied by a fruit jelly or fruit cheese and gravy made from their own juices, thickened with a little flour. The grey wild partridge with a chestnut horseshoe on his breast is the most delicious of all gamebirds. Roast with a parsnip, then suck the meat from the bones until the juice dribbles down your chin. All that should remain is a heap of bones on your plate. Some falconers say that partridge or grouse that has been hawked tastes far better than one that has been shot. This is possibly due to the adrenalin pumping through their bodies while being hunted by the falcon; pluck such birds while warm and eat within the hour. We have certainly found this to be true with grouse hawked by a falconer friend, Roger Upton. However, our adrenalin pumps quite well also when he feeds to the pointers the grouse that are surplus to the day's eating requirements – what a waste! Older birds and venison are very often rather dry, so it is necessary to make a rich sauce. All the recipes given here have some sort of sauce which acts as an insurance against disaster should the meat not stand up in its own right.

Venison is easily obtained nowadays, and is relatively cheap compared with something like beef. The adult stag has better meat because it carries more fat. Many butchers are licensed to deal in game and registered game dealers advertise in business directories. They will guide and advise you on all aspects of game and how best to cook and enjoy it. I thoroughly recommend obtaining game only through reputable dealers to ensure top quality meat.

Cooking game is largely a matter of your own imagination and of adapting favourite recipes to suit you. The following are a few ideas more usually used to prepare other meats but which can be equally successful with game.

Squirrel Pie   Not the darling red squirrel, I hasten to add, but the aggressive grey which, since its introduction to Britain, has been classified as vermin due to the tremendous amount of damage it does to young trees. However, it is extremely succulent, tasting rather like gamey rabbit or chicken. Various members of my family have enjoyed eating squirrel in many different ways, but, being quite difficult to shoot, there are none in my freezer at the moment. Use any rabbit or chicken recipe.

Rook Pie   Use a recipe for chicken and add mushrooms and chopped parsley. The bones and meat make a wonderful jelly. Top the pie with rough puff pastry and eat cold with some redcurrant jelly. The manner in which they are shot was once described to a friend of mine, who, on hearing that the young rooks advance in a line along the tree branch and are shot with one cartridge, exclaimed that they arrange themselves in 'a pie group'.

Rack of Red Deer   Roast as you would a lamb and serve with a bullace cheese, or fruit jelly, some pommes boulangère and tiny peas or mange-tout.

Woodcock   The head of the bird can be twisted round and the bill spiked through the body, holding it in place like a skewer. It is best cooked as described on page 88.

Collared Dove   Some people have been misled into eating collared dove, thinking it is quail. Served with a delicate sauce and Muscat grapes it makes a delicious dish.

Wild Pig   My family has eaten wild pig sausages with beans and mash and found them to be very good. The rest of the animal was dealt with like pork and tastes slightly stronger.

Pheasant on Watercress

Serves 6   Preparation time: 15 minutes   Cooking time: 45 minutes

This pheasant is served warm – it is a delicious way to use up frozen pheasant in the summer. I always wish I could eat the sleek, fat birds I see strutting in the late summer but I daresay, being wily birds of many seasons, they would be rather tough.

Brace of pheasants
275ml/¹/₂ pint vinaigrette (see page
  174)
3 eggs, hard-boiled
1 shallot, finely chopped
2 bunches watercress

1 Roast the pheasant in the usual way, with some bacon over the breast and a little extra butter for basting.

2 Make a thick vinaigrette by adding 3 yolks of hard-boiled eggs and a finely chopped shallot to the basic recipe.

3 Arrange the watercress on a large platter.

4 Carve the pheasant thinly and place on top of the watercress. Pour the vinaigrette over the pheasant and serve immediately.

Serving suggestion: You could follow this course with some very creamy pommes boulangère, or serve them at the side on flat cocotte dishes.

Pheasant à la Normande

Serves 8   Preparation time: 10 minutes   Cooking time: 45 minutes

This is a more simple method of dealing with the classic recipe. You can use home-made apple purée from your freezer or a jar from the supermarket.

Brace of pheasants
275ml/10fl oz water or pheasant
  stock from a previous roast
Calvados
6 – 8 tablespoons apple pureé
150ml/¼ pint single cream
Parsley

1 Roast the pheasants in a pan with the water or stock. When cooked, remove, carve and keep warm and well covered on a meat platter.

2 Return the roasting pan to the heat and boil the liquid rapidly, stirring so that all the juices are well mixed. Add the juices from the carving.

3 Pour in a glass of calvados and boil for 1 minute. Stir in enough apple purée to make the sauce of the desired consistency and add the cream. Adjust the seasoning, add some more calvados to taste and pour into a warm sauceboat or jug.

Serving suggestion: Garnish the pheasant with parsley and decorate with feathers. Hand round the sauce separately.

Chinese Pheasant

Serves 8   Preparation time: Marinade overnight   Cooking time: 15 minutes

Towards the end of the shooting season, pheasants have been cooked every which way. At this time they can be bought fairly cheaply and are usually more economic, weight for weight, than chicken. This dish can be prepared well in advance and kept warm or re-heated from cold. If it is to be kept warm, make sure that it is well sealed with greaseproof paper, foil and a lid. Use the remaining meat and carcass to make a casserole or a nourishing lunchtime soup.

8 breasts from 2 brace of pheasants
Dry sherry
2 – 3 tablespoons soy sauce
3 tablespoons sunflower oil
275g/10oz ginger, fresh and grated
5 cloves garlic
100g/4oz tin black beans in sauce
Vegetable stock
5 tablespoons chervil, chopped

1 Shred the flesh into finger-sized strips. (The wing can also be used if necessary.) Marinade overnight in enough dry sherry to cover and 2–3 tablespoons soy sauce.

2 After 24 hours, heat the oil in a large pan and fry the ginger and garlic for a few minutes. Add the strips of meat and sauté for a further 5 minutes. Add the beans and warm them through. Add enough stock to cover all the ingredients and simmer for a further 5 minutes, or until cooked.

Serving suggestion: Serve in a casserole or similar dish with chervil scattered over the top. Serve with plain rice or, more extravagantly, wild rice and a green salad.

Woodcock

Serves 1   Preparation time: 5 minutes   Cooking time: 15 minutes

A shy and beautiful bird of our woodlands, if you are lucky you can catch a glimpse of their seemingly erratic behaviour in spring marking out their territory, called roding, prior to courtship, to make the hen enthusiastic. In my opinion they are much too special to eat, but for those who wish to, they are best eaten before Christmas. They live on a diet of berries and insects. To prepare for roasting the head is twisted so that the bill acts as a skewer and pierces the body to hold the bird together. Traditionally they are cooked undrawn. Allow one bird per person.

Woodcock
2 rashers bacon
Slice of bread, toasted
Seasoning

Preheat the oven to 220°C/425°F/ Gas Mark 7.

1 Place the woodcock in a roasting pan, cover with strips of bacon and cook at 220°C/425°F/Gas Mark 7 for 15 minutes or so.

2 When cooked, remove from the oven, throw away the gizzards and mash up the trail with a fork. Season and heat again with the pan juices.

Serving suggestion: Spread the paste on to some toast, place the woodcock on top and eat immediately.

Note: Some people add a dash of lemon juice and brandy to the paste, and some add pâté.

Partridge with Tarragon

Serves 6   Preparation time: 20 minutes   Cooking time: 30 minutes

Although a young gamebird is delicious plain roasted, you could try this method of French roasting with older birds which involves braising on a bed of vegetables in a deep casserole. Pheasant benefits from this method, becoming particularly succulent.

Brace of partridge
100g/4oz butter
2 carrots, sliced
1 onion, sliced
2 – 3 teaspoons dried tarragon or 20
  fresh leaves
Salt and pepper
Stock
Wine glass of Madeira

Pre-heat the oven to 200°C/400°F/ Gas Mark 6.

1 Brown the birds in 50g/2oz butter in a frying pan. Discard the butter since it inevitably browns and will spoil the flavour of the sauce.

2 Melt a further 50g/2oz butter in a deep casserole and sauté the vegetables for a few minutes. Add the herbs and season well. Place the birds on the top, cover them in foil and bake for 30 minutes, for a young bird, 200°C/400°F/ Gas Mark 6.

3 When cooked remove the birds, carve and keep them warm.

4 Purée the vegetables in a blender or vegetable mill.

5 Pour a little stock into the casserole and place it over the heat, stirring well to mix in all the juices from the roasting. Add the puréed vegetables and more stock until the sauce reaches the desired consistency. Add the Madeira, adjust the seasoning and add extra fresh herbs as desired. Pour the sauce over the meat and garnish with parsley.

Serving Suggestions: This dish will keep for at least 45 minutes without spoiling if well covered.

Haunch of Roe

Serves 8   Preparation time: 10–15minutes   Cooking time: 1 hour   Marinade: 4 hours

Roe is not as readily available as other venison and is therefore a great treat.

1.5kg/3lb haunch of roe
½ bottle red vermouth
1 onion, sliced
1 celery stick, sliced
3 carrots, sliced
12 peppercorns
225g/8oz bacon rashers
50g/2oz butter
50g/2oz flour
Juice and rind of 1 orange
2 tablespoons redcurrant jelly
1 glass port
Seasoning

1 Marinade the haunch in the vermouth for 4 hours.

2 Sit the haunch on the braising vegetables, add water to marinade and cover with bacon. Cook for 1 hour for pink flesh and longer for grey. Remove, carve and keep warm.

3 Make the sauce by draining off the braising vegetables and discarding them. Boil the liquid to reduce to 575ml/1pint. Mix the softened butter and the flour together. Add to the liquor and stir until thickened. Add the orange juice and rind, jelly and port. Re-heat and adjust seasoning to taste.

Serving suggestion: Serve at once with the sauce served separately.

Redcurrant Pot of Venison

Serves 4   Preparation time: 5 minutes   Cooking time: 15 minutes

4–8 venison chops
8oz/225g redcurrant jelly
Seasoning
150ml/¼ pint water
Parsley

Pre-heat oven to 220°C/425°F/Gas Mark 7.

---

1 Arrange the venison chops in a roasting tin or earthenware dish. Spread them liberally with the redcurrant jelly. Season and add the water.

---

2 Bake at 220°C/425°F/Gas Mark 7 for about 15 minutes. (The cooking time will vary according to the thickness of the chops.)

Serving suggestion: Serve immediately, spooning over the delicious sauce and scattering the parsley on top.

Roast Saddle of Hare in Brandy and Cream

Serves 4–6   Preparation time: 10 minutes   Cooking time: 45–50 minutes
Marinade: 8 hours

A very succulent dish, this can be served with wild rice and a plain green salad.

1 saddle of hare
3 glasses red wine
4 tablespoons olive oil
8 juniper berries
Mixed herbs
Parsley stalks
50g/2oz butter, melted
1 glass Cognac
150ml/¼ pint double cream
Parsley, chopped

Pre-heat the oven to 230°C/450°F/Gas Mark 8.

1   Marinade the hare in 2 glasses of the red wine, olive oil, juniper berries, herbs and parsley stalks for about 8 hours. (This could be prepared in the morning prior to serving in the evening.) Baste frequently. After 8 hours or so, pat dry with kitchen paper.

2   Tear off the membrane and brush the saddle with melted butter. Sear the meat in a very hot oven 230°C/450°F/Gas Mark 8 for 10 minutes. Reduce the oven heat to 200°C/400°F/Gas Mark 6.

3   Meanwhile heat the strained marinade, pour into the roasting dish with the hare and cook for 35 minutes at 200°C/400°F/Gas Mark 6, basting frequently.

4   When the hare is cooked, lift out of the dish, carve and keep warm. Pour the brandy and last glass of wine into the remaining pan juices and stir well. Add the cream and re-heat until the liquid has thickened.

Serving suggestion: Pour the sauce on to the hare and scatter with parsley to serve.

Saddle of Fallow
in Orange Sauce

Serves 8   Preparation time: 10 minutes   Cooking time: Approximately 1 hour
30 minutes   Marinade: 3–4 hours.

This is an unusual way of treating fallow but ensures that the meat does not dry
out with cooking.

1.5–2kg/3–4lb saddle of fallow
Red wine
Oil
Peppercorns
Jar of honey
2 cartons condensed orange juice
150ml/¼ pint water

Pre-heat the oven to 200°C/400°F/Gas Mark 6

---

1 Marinade the haunch for 3–4 hours in a marinade made up of the wine, oil
and peppercorns.

---

2 Spread the haunch with honey and cover it lightly with foil. Bake for 20
minutes per 450g/1lb at 200°C/400°F/Gas Mark 6.

---

3 When cooked, remove and carve. Keep warm.

---

4 Pour the orange juice on to the meat juices and honey. Add water and boil,
stirring well. Allow to reduce until of a thick consistency. Season and pour
into a jug.

Serving suggestion: Serve with the orange sauce passed around separately.

Pigeon and Rabbit Terrine

Serves 8   Preparation time: 30 minutes   Cooking time: 1 hour 30 minutes

This has the virtue of keeping for at least a week in the refrigerator. It does shrink from the sides of the container, but looks very attractive when served on to the plate.

12 rashers bacon
225g/8oz lamb's liver
225g/8oz sausage meat
1 large onion, chopped
6 tablespoons parsley, chopped
1 egg and 50ml/2fl oz milk, mixed
   together
6 tablespoons breadcrumbs
Seasoning
Port or brandy
Rabbit
Pigeon
Bay-leaves

Pre-heat the oven to 180°C/350°F/Gas Mark 4.

1 Line a terrine with the bacon, reserving some for the top.

2 Mash or blend together the livers and sausage meat. Mix well with the onions, parsley, egg and milk and breadcrumbs. Season well and add the port or brandy.

3 Place half the mixture in the terrine. Press strips of rabbit and pigeon into the mixture. Cover with the remaining mixture and press down well. Decorate the top with bay-leaves and cover with the remaining bacon. Cover with foil and cook in a bain-marie for 1½ hours at 180°C/350°F/Gas Mark 4.

4 When cooked, leave to cool overnight, with weights on top to compress the mixture. Remove the bay-leaves before serving.

Serving suggestion: Turn into a bowl or on to a plate and serve with toast or French bread.

Savernake Pigeon Pie

Serves 6   Preparation time: 25 minutes   Cooking time: 4 hours

This is best made the day before it is required so that the birds cool in the liquid. They can be re-heated before serving. They will be so tender that they will fall apart to the touch. This is a very rich dish and should be followed by a fruit salad or compôte of fruit.

6 pigeon
Butter
2 carrots, sliced
2 onions, chopped
2 potatoes, sliced
2 celery sticks, sliced
Stock
Seasoning
Port (optional)
Parsley

Pre-heat the oven to 180°C/350°F/Gas Mark 4.

1 Brown the birds all over in the butter using a large frying pan.

2 Put all the vegetables into a deep casserole and place the birds in upside-down. Pour on stock to half-way up the birds and bring to the boil. After 2 hours turn the birds up the right way.

3 Cook the birds at 180°C/350°F/Gas Mark 4 for 3–4 hours. Leave them overnight to cool in their own liquid.

4 Roll out the pastry and cut into circles with a 7.5cm/3in round cutter. Bake at 200°C/400°F/Gas Mark 6 for 5 minutes.

5 Lift the birds from the liquor, and purée the liquor and vegetables. Return to the pan and re-heat. Adjust the seasoning and add the port, if desired. Decorate with parsley and top with the pastry circles at the last minute.

Serving suggestion: Serve with mashed potato.

Chapter 7
TRADITIONAL LUNCHEON AND NURSERY PUDDINGS

Plums in a Veil	98
Rhubarb and Banana Meringue	99
Sarah's Mulberry Pie	100
Queen of Puddings	101
Emily Astor's Pudding	102
Monmouth Pudding	103
Mama's Treacle Duff	104
Hot Chocolate Pots	105
Apple Almond Meringue	106
Brown Bread Ice-Cream	107
Sarah's Lemon Meringue Pie	108
Summer Pudding	109
Cedric's Favourite	110
Balaclava Bananas	111
Marmalade Meringue	112
Apple Amber Pudding	113
A Charlotte	114
Treacle Tart	115
Bread and Butter Pudding	116
Crisped Frog-Spawn and Apple	117
Lemon Layer	118
Junket	119

I have divided the puddings into three chapters – nursery and traditional puddings for lunchtimes; desserts which are suitable for dinner parties (although all the dishes can be served at any time); and quick and rich dishes for really speedy puddings or desserts.

I always make a pudding for a dinner party. Apart from the fact that it is fattening (usually) and cheaper than cheese, I would feel terribly cheated if I wasn't offered a pudding when dining out, even if only for supper. In addition, I always make fruit salad or sliced oranges and a few petits pots de chocolat to have with the main pudding. Generally people eat a bit of everything, which proves a point. Girls who say they never eat pudding do, and only one I know of has never weakened, and that is Annie who must be mentioned for her fortitude. (She supplied the receipe 'Annie Bruce's Pasta'.)

Many of the following recipes have been chosen from the nursery lunch repertoire. There are Sunday lunch puddings and traditional puddings such as treacle tart. Most nursery lunch puddings will go anywhere, as they say, and are usually great favourites with men who become quite nostalgic at the sight of a really good bread and butter pudding. A friend of mine is always daring me to make semolina with grated chocolate for a grand dinner party but so far I haven't been brave enough. It is because of the children that so many puds have been tried and lunch is often as much of an institution as tea in our family.

Very simple for a summer lunch is an uncooked, glazed fruit tart. My own version might be made with pâté Sucrée (short and sweet pastry) but an ordinary shortcrust pastry will do, pressed into a flan dish and baked blind. When it is cool, fill it with any fresh fruits in season arranged decoratively. Finally glaze the fruit by brushing with melted apricot jam or redcurrant jelly. It is so easy to make and delightful to eat. It could be served with crème fraiche or unpasteurised cream.

Plums in a Veil

Serves 6   Preparation time: 25 minutes   Cooking time: 10 minutes

This can also be made with apple but plums or damsons give a more distinctive flavour.

700g/2lb plums, damsons or
  cherries
50g/2oz butter
100g/4oz breadcrumbs
50g/2oz demerara sugar
275ml/¹/₂ pint double cream,
  whipped
Extra soft brown or caster sugar

1 Cook the fruit in a pan, and stir over the heat until soft. Remove, allow to cool and take out the stones.

2 Melt the butter in a large frying pan and add the breadcrumbs. Fry until golden. Add the sugar, stirring well. Remove after 1 minute and allow to cool.

3 Using a glass bowl and starting with the fruit, make several alternate layers with the breadcrumbs. Finish with the cream, which should be spooned on and lightly smoothed.

4 Scatter a layer of sugar on top and put under the grill until the sugar caramelises.

Serving suggestion: Serve well chilled.

Rhubarb and Banana Meringue

Serves 6   Preparation time: 20 minutes   Cooking time: 10 minutes

An unusual way of dealing with the seasonal glut of rhubarb.

450g/1lb rhubarb
Caster sugar to taste
4 bananas, puréed
3 egg-whites, whipped stiffly
3 tablespoons caster sugar

Pre-heat the oven to 130°C/250°F/Gas Mark ½.

1 Cook the rhubarb with sugar to taste and pour into a fireproof dish. Pour on a layer of banana.

2 Whisk the whites stiffly and beat in the sugar. Spread over the fruits and bake at 130°C/250°F/Gas Mark ½ until crisp.

Serving suggestion: Serve immediately.

Sarah's Mulberry Pie

Serves 6   Preparation time: 15 minutes   Cooking time: 30 minutes

An Anglicised version of an American pudding.

50g/2oz butter
250g/9oz shortbread, crushed
75g/3oz ground almonds
50g/2oz caster sugar
1 egg
4 tablespoons redcurrant jelly
1 tablespoon arrowroot
700g/2lb mulberries or
  redcurrants
Cream to serve

Pre-heat the oven to 200°C/400°F/Gas Mark 6.

1 Melt the butter in a saucepan and stir in the shortbread, ground almonds, sugar and egg.

2 Put half this mixture into the bottom of a fireproof dish of approximately 18cm/7in circumference.

3 Melt the redcurrant jelly, stir in the arrowroot and continue stirring over the heat until thickened. Mix with the mulberries or redcurrants and put into the fireproof dish. Top with the remaining pie mixture and bake in the oven at 200°C/400°F/Gas Mark 6 for 30 minutes until golden.

Serving suggestion: Serve with cream.

Queen of Puddings

Serves 6   Preparation time: 20 minutes   Cooking time: 1 hour

So delicious, you could serve this for dinner.

50g/2oz butter
8 tablespoons caster sugar
Grated rind of 2 large lemons
150g/5oz breadcrumbs
575ml/1 pint milk, heated
3 eggs
4–5 tablespoons jam

Pre-heat the oven to 180°C/350°F/Gas Mark 4.

1 Beat the butter and sugar until fluffy, reserving 2 tablespoons sugar for the meringue, and add the lemon rind.

2 Soak the breadcrumbs in the milk for 10 minutes. Stir all these ingredients together and beat in the egg-yolks.

3 Pour into a buttered, shallow ovenproof dish and bake at 180°C/350°F/Gas Mark 4 until set, about 35 minutes. Allow to cool and spread with jam. Reduce the oven temperature to 140°C/275°F/Gas Mark 1.

4 Beat the egg-whites until stiff, fold in 2 tablespoons of sugar and whisk again. Spread the meringue over the pudding and bake at 140°C/275°F/Gas Mark 1 until set and golden, about 25 minutes.

Serving suggestion: Serve immediately.

Emily Astor's Pudding

Serves 6   Preparation time: 20 minutes   Cooking time: 20 minutes

Emily is six and sometimes makes the topping for the pudding when we have a nursery lunch with the Astors. It is a very original way of dealing with the annual autumnal glut of cooking apples. I have often made this for family Sunday lunch.

450g/1lb apples, peeled and sliced
Sugar to taste
75g/3oz butter
6 heaped tablespoons golden syrup
175g/6oz cornflakes
Cream to serve

Pre-heat the oven to 200°C/400°F/Gas Mark 6.

1 Cook the apples in a pan until soft, with sugar to taste. When cooked, place them in a shallow heatproof dish and keep them warm.

2 Melt the butter in a saucepan, add the syrup and cook over the heat, stirring until they are well mixed together.

3 Remove from the heat and stir in the cornflakes until all are coated. Spoon on to the apples and bake in the oven at 200°C/400°F/Gas Mark 6 for about 10 minutes, until the top is browned.

Serving suggestion: Serve hot with cream.

Monmouth Pudding

Serves 6   Preparation time: 20 minutes   Cooking time: 35 minutes

Another Sunday lunch recipe – this one is from Jane Torday's *A Little Old-Fashioned Book of Nursery Recipes*, and, as she suggests, it should be made in an ovenproof, transparent dish because it is so pretty. I use raspberry jam – slightly less than the recipe indicates.

150ml/¼ pint hot milk
100g/4oz white breadcrumbs
50g/2oz soft butter
50g/2oz sugar
Grated peel of 1 lemon
2 egg-whites, beaten stiffly
4 tablespoons jam
Double cream to serve

Pre-heat the oven to 180°C/350°F/Gas Mark 4.

1   Pour hot milk on the breadcrumbs and leave for 15 minutes.

2   Cream the butter and sugar and beat into the breadcrumb mixture.

3   Flavour the mixture with lemon zest. Fold in the egg-whites.

4   Butter a deep Pyrex dish and pour in half the breadcrumb mixture, then a thick layer of jam, then the rest of the breadcrumbs.

5   Cover with buttered foil and stand in a baking tray with enough water in it to come half-way up the side of the dish. Cook in the oven for 30 minutes at 180°C/350°F/Gas Mark 4.

Serving suggestion: Serve with cream.

Mama's Treacle Duff

Serves 6   Preparation time: 15 minutes   Cooking time: 1 hour 30 minutes

When we were children we called this 'peacle duff' and perhaps it should be still. It sticks to the roof of your mouth in the most glorious way.

175g/6oz self-raising flour
100g/4oz suet
1 teaspoon sugar
Pinch of salt
Water
25g/1oz butter
450g/1lb golden syrup
Cream to serve

Pre-heat the oven to 190°C/375°F/Gas Mark 4.

1 Make a rollable dough with the flour, suet, sugar, salt and water.

2 Butter a pudding basin and fill one-quarter of it with golden syrup.

3 Put the dough into the basin, cover with foil and weight with a saucepan lid.

4 Put the basin into a bain-marie or roasting dish filled with hot water. Cook in the bottom of the oven for 1 hour 30 minutes at 190°C/375°F/Gas Mark 4.

Serving suggestion: Serve with the remaining warmed syrup and cream.

Hot Chocolate Pots

Serves 4   Preparation time: 10 minutes   Cooking time: 15 minutes

A slightly cakey soufflé – foolproof to make. When we eat this we take one spoonful from the middle, eat it and then pour some cream in the hole.

2 eggs, beaten
3 tablespoons caster sugar
2 tablespoons cocoa
1 teaspoon baking powder
Cream to serve

Pre-heat the oven to 200°C/400°F/Gas Mark 6.

1 Beat the eggs and sugar together. Sieve the cocoa and baking powder and fold them together.

2 Pour into 4 buttered ramekins to the half-way mark, to allow them to rise.

3 Bake in the oven at 200°C/400°F/Gas Mark 6 for 15 minutes.

Serving suggestion: Serve immediately with cream.

Apple Almond Meringue

Serves 4   Preparation time: 20 minutes   Cooking time: 10 minutes

Sometimes I use more of all these ingredients and start with a layer of pulped apple, then fruits, then meringue. The meringue is rather cakey and is equally delicious served cold.

6 apples, peeled and cored
1 glass red wine
100g/4oz sugar
100g/4oz crystallised fruits soaked
  in Cointreau
4 eggs, separated
75g/3oz caster sugar
75g/3oz ground almonds

Pre-heat the oven to 200°C/400°F/Gas Mark 6.

1 Using a saucepan, poach the apples in the wine and sugar. Do not allow them to collapse.

2 Put the apples into a heatproof dish and fill the holes with crystallised fruits.

3 Beat the yolks and sugar until fluffy. Stir in the almonds, beat the egg-whites until stiff and fold them into the mixture. Pour over the apples.

4 Bake in the oven at 200°C/400°F/Gas Mark 6 for 10 minutes until pale golden.

Serving suggestion: Serve with cream.

Brown Bread Ice-Cream

Serves 6   Preparation time: 1 hour   Cooking time: 10 minutes

This is best made on the morning of your dinner party, as the breadcrumbs will remain crunchy for about 12 hours.

275ml/½ pint double cream,
  whipped
4 egg-whites
50g/2oz caster sugar, flavoured
  with a few drops of vanilla
50g/2oz butter
175g/6oz soft brown sugar
175g/6oz brown breadcrumbs

1 Whip the cream and then whip the egg-whites until stiff. Fold them together with the caster sugar. Put in a bowl in the freezer and stir three times, once every 20 minutes.

2 Fry the butter, brown sugar and breadcrumbs together until they make a toffee crunch. Allow to cool.

3 Stir into the freezing ice-cream mixture at the third stir.

4 Put the mixture into individual pots or one plastic container and leave in the freezer.

Serving suggestion: Remove from the freezer about 10 minutes before eating.

Sarah's Lemon Meringue Pie

Serves 6   Preparation time: 20 minutes   Cooking time: 20 minutes

Apparently, as a child, my husband called this 'orang-utang pie' and fervently thanked that large animal whenever he came across him in the Natural History Museum. Lemon meringue pie is a great favourite for all of us and this recipe from our mother's help is the best I have ever tasted. It is not necessary to serve it with cream.

100g/4oz short pastry
175g/6oz caster sugar
Grated rind and juice of 2 lemons
250ml/9fl oz water
3 tablespoons arrowroot, dissolved
  in 2 tablespoons water
3 eggs, separated

Pre-heat the oven to 200°C/400°F/Gas Mark 6.

1   Roll pastry thinly and bake blind in a 20cm/8in flan tin for 10 minutes in the oven at 200°C/400°F/Gas Mark 6. Reduce the oven temperature to 180°C/350°F/Gas Mark 4.

2   Place half of the sugar, the lemon rind, juice and water in a pan over the heat and stir until the sugar dissolves.

3   Stir in the arrowroot until thickened, remove from the heat and allow to cool. Beat in the egg-yolks.

4   Pour on to the pastry and bake at 180°C/350°F/Gas Mark 4 until the filling forms a skin (approximately 5 minutes).

5   Beat the egg-whites to a froth, fold in the rest of the sugar and whisk until stiff. Cover the lemon with the meringue mixture and bake in the oven at 180°C/350°F/Gas Mark 4 until golden (approximately 20 minutes).

Serving suggestion: Serve warm.

Summer Pudding

Serves 8   Preparation time: 20 minutes   Cooking time: 5 minutes

Almost everybody's favourite, so a pudding which had to be included in this collection.

Large white loaf, sliced
225g/8oz redcurrants
225g/8oz blackcurrants
225g/8oz raspberries
225g/8oz cherries, pitted (a tin will
   do)
Sugar to taste
Cream to serve

1 Squash the slices into a pudding basin and line it completely.

2 Stew all the fruit with some sugar to taste. Sieve the fruit to obtain a mug full of juices to reserve. Pour the fruit and juices into the pudding basin and cover with a lid of bread.

3 Cover with a plate and weight with whatever is to hand.

4 Refrigerate overnight. Turn out on to a plate and pour over the reserved juice.

Serving suggestion: Serve with thick cream.

Cedric's Favourite

Serves 6   Preparation time: 10 minutes   Cooking time: 20 minutes

This was a particular favourite of my husband's grandfather, the Marquess of Ailesbury. The old cook used rough puff pastry instead of Fillo leaves, and currants and sultanas mixed with brown sugar in place of the mincemeat. You can always do the same if you haven't the exact ingredients.

6 Fillo leaves
50g/2oz butter, melted
450g/1lb jar of traditional
  mincemeat
2 medium-sized Cox's apples,
  peeled
2 tablespoons brandy
Icing sugar
Cream to serve

Pre-heat the oven to 200°C/400°F/Gas Mark 6.

1 Lay the Fillo leaves on a baking tray and brush each layer with the melted butter. Spread mincemeat up the middle, leaving the edges clear for pinching the pastry later.

2 Grate the peeled apples over the top and sprinkle with brandy.

3 Pinch together the sides and ends and brush with more butter. Score the top with vents to allow steam to escape.

4 Bake in the oven at 200°C/400°F/Gas Mark 6 for approximately 20 minutes, or until golden-brown.

5 Dust with icing sugar and cut off the unattractive ends before serving.

Serving suggestion: Serve with thick cream.

Balaclava Bananas

Serves 6   Preparation and cooking time: 20 minutes

I named this pudding in deference to my husband's illustrious ancestor who amongst other things went to war in the Crimea on his yacht!

100g/4oz butter
100g/4oz soft brown sugar
6 bananas, peeled
Cointreau
Cream to serve

1 Melt the butter and sugar in a large frying pan.

2 Add the bananas and cook on a low heat until soft and caked in the toffee which the butter and sugar have made.

3 Pour on Cointreau to taste.

Serving suggestion: Serve straight from the pan on to hot plates with a blob of cream on each serving.

Marmalade Meringue

Serves 8   Preparation time: 15 minutes   Cooking time: 50 minutes

A delicious Sunday lunch pudding following game – all the better if the marmalade is home-made and a rich dark brown colour. I sometimes stir in some Cointreau to the mixture before baking.

175g/6oz short pastry
3 eggs, separated
450g/1lb mature marmalade
Cream to serve

Pre-heat the oven to 180°C/350°F/Gas Mark 4.

1 Line a 30cm/12in flan tin with thinly rolled pastry and bake blind at 200°C/400°F/Gas Mark 6 for 15 minutes.

2 Beat the egg-yolks and marmalade together. Spoon into the pastry and bake at 180°C/350°F/Gas Mark 4 for 15 minutes or until set.

3 Whisk the egg-whites until stiff, fold in the sugar and spoon on to the marmalade mixture. Bake for 20 minutes.

Serving suggestion: Serve hot with cream.

Apple Amber Pudding

Serves 6   Preparation time: 30 minutes   Cooking time: 45 minutes

This is one of my favourite puddings.

100g/4oz short pastry
450g/1lb Cox's apples, peeled and
  cored
75g/3oz sugar
50g/2oz butter
1 lemon
2 eggs, separated
50g/2oz caster sugar

Pre-heat the oven to 200°C/400°F/Gas Mark 6.

1 Bake pastry blind in flan dish, 20cm/8in in diameter.

2 Stew the apples with the sugar, butter and lemon rind and juice. When soft, beat in the yolks. Pour into the flan base and bake at 200°C/400°F/Gas Mark 6 for 30 minutes, or until the mixture sets. Reduce the oven temperature to 150°C/200°F/Gas Mark 4.

3 Meanwhile beat the egg-whites until stiff, fold in the sugar and beat again.

4 Top the apple mixture with the meringue and bake at 150°C/200°F/Gas Mark 4 for 15 minutes, until golden.

Serving suggestion: Serve immediately.

A Charlotte

Serves 8   Preparation time: 20 minutes   Chilling time: Overnight

Large packet of sponge fingers
3 tablespoons marmalade
3 tablespoons brandy
575ml/1 pint double cream,
  whipped
Lemon juice and sugar to taste

---

1 Line a 20cm/8in soufflé dish with the fingers, or split them in half lengthways and across and line ramekins.

---

2 Mix the remaining ingredients together and pour into the dish or dishes. Leave to chill overnight.

Serving suggestion: Turn out and serve with warmed, puréed marmalade.

Treacle Tart

Serves 6   Prepartion time: 10 minutes   Cooking time: 20 minutes

This is the sort of recipe I make without measuring the ingredients and so the results may vary, probably according to the freshness or otherwise of the bread. I like to serve this warm and it must be extremely syrupy.

175g/6oz short pastry
Rice
100g/4oz white breadcrumbs
7 generous tablespoons golden syrup
Juice and grated rind of 1 lemon
Cream to serve

Pre-heat the oven to 200°C/400°F/Gas Mark 6.

1 Line a 20cm/8in tin with the short pastry. Prick well with a fork. Line this base with greaseproof paper and fill with rice. Bake for 10 minutes on 200°C/ 400°F/Gas Mark 6. Remove from the oven and remove the greaseproof paper with the rice.

2 Mix the rest of the ingredients together and fill the pastry base. Bake for a further 10 minutes.

Serving suggestion: Serve with whipped cream.

Bread and Butter Pudding

Serves 4–6   Preparation time: 15 minutes   Cooking time: 15 minutes

Unlike most recipes for bread and butter pudding this is essentially light and not soggy. The custard is creamy and the top is very crisp. It is best eaten at once, but it will keep in a warming oven for about an hour.

2 eggs
275ml/¹/₂ pint single cream
150ml/¹/₄ pint milk
10 slices thick white bread, cut into
    quarters
Butter
2 tablespoons demerara sugar
50g/2oz mixed dried fruit, sprinkled
    with sherry
Custard

Pre-heat the oven to 200°C/400°F/Gas Mark 6.

1 Beat the eggs, cream and milk together until smooth. Butter the bread sparingly.

2 Lightly butter an 850ml/1½ pint dish. Layer the bread into the dish, buttered side up, and sprinkle each layer with demerara sugar, fruit and a layer of custard. Press down with a spoon.

3 Pour on the remaining custard and top with a final layer of bread and sugar. Bake at 200°C/400°F/Gas Mark 6 for about 15 minutes or until the top is crisp and golden.

Serving suggestion: Serve immediately with thick cream.

116

Crisped Frog-Spawn and Apple

Serves 6   Preparation time: 20 minutes   Cooking time: 40 minutes

A much maligned milk pudding, this is, however, a great favourite with children and adults alike – just don't tell the latter till later! This one is a sort of souffléd crumble with a difference. I nearly always use Cox's apples for their flavour but cooking apples will do, as long as you remember to add sugar. You will also need a bain-marie or a large roasting pan half-filled with hot water.

450g/1lb apples, peeled, cored and
*   sliced*
100g/4oz butter
75g/3oz fresh white breadcrumbs
40g/1½oz brown sugar
Cinnamon to taste
50g/2oz seed pearl tapioca
450ml/1pint milk
50g/2oz white sugar
A few drops vanilla essence
2 eggs, separated

Pre-heat the oven to 180°C/350°F/Gas Mark 4.

1 Arrange the apples neatly in a lightly buttered 1 litre/2 pint soufflé dish.

2 Place 65g/2½oz butter, the breadcrumbs, brown sugar and cinnamon into a frying pan and fry until golden. Place on top of the apples.

3 Place the tapioca, milk, white sugar, vanilla essence and 25g/1oz butter into a saucepan and simmer for at least 15 minutes. Stir until thickened. Remove from the heat and beat in the egg-yolks. Whisk the egg-whites until they are stiff and fold into the mixture.

4 Spoon the liquid mixture on to the apples. Place the dish in a bain-marie and bake in the oven at 180°C/350°F/Gas Mark 4 for 40 minutes.

Serving suggestion: Serve immediately.

Lemon Layer

Serves 6   Preparation time: 10 minutes   Cooking time: 30 minutes

This recipe uses another much maligned ingredient – semolina. The dish has a light cake topping with a strong lemon cream underneath – far superior to the usual lemon layer pudding made with flour.

2 eggs, separated
300ml/11fl oz milk
50g/2oz butter
100g/4oz sugar
Juice and rind of 2 lemons
50g/2oz semolina
Cream to serve

Pre-heat the oven to 200°C/400°F/Gas Mark 6.

1 Beat the egg-yolks with the milk. Heat the butter, sugar, lemon juice and rind until the sugar dissolves. Stir in the semolina and beat in the milk and egg mixture until it is smooth.

2 Whip the egg-whites until they are stiff and fold them into the mixture. Pour into a buttered 850ml/1½ pint soufflé dish and bake at 200°C/400°F/Gas Mark 6 for 30 minutes.

Serving suggestion: Serve hot with cream.

Junket

Serves 4   Preparation time: 10 minutes   Cooking time: 1 minute

Made with cream this becomes a sort of crème fraîche and is delicious with stewed fruit or a thick layer of grated chocolate.

575ml/1pint single cream
1 teaspoon caster sugar
1 teaspoon rennet
Grated nutmeg (optional)
225g/8oz chocolate menier grated

1 Warm the cream, stir in the sugar until it has dissolved. Stir in the rennet.

2 Pour into a shallow 575ml/1 pint dish or ramekins and leave for several hours until set.

Serving suggestion: Serve chilled with a sprinkling of nutmeg or a thick layer of grated chocolate.

CHAPTER 8

JUST DESSERTS FOR DINNER PARTIES

Anne-Marie Stehlin's Compôte of Figs	122
Surprise au Grand Marnier	123
Figs, Raspberries and Cream	124
A Grand Soufflé	125
Soufflé Rothschild	126
Chocolate Meringue Bombe	127
Oranges in Kirsch	128
Bill's Bowl of Strawberries	129
Plums in a Jar	130
Chocolate Flatlet	131
Apple Crack	132
Iced Pears and Passion-Fruit	133
Kissel	134
Damp Almond Cake	135
Crème Asphodèle	136
Petits Pots de Chocolat au Rhum	137
Chocolate Soufflé	138
Compôte of Fruits	139
Baked Stuffed Peaches	140
Louise's Poached Pears	141
Caramelised Cox's	142
Bombe Savernake	143
Sunken Strawberries	144
Crêpes	145
Crêpes Suzette	146
Crêpes Stuffed with Cherries	147
Crêpes Stuffed with Pears	148
Crêpes Normandes	149
Pear Feuilleté	150
Crème Brûleé	151
Crème Caramel	152

It is interesting to note that by the early nineteenth century, upper servants such as butlers and housekeepers would leave the servants' hall to eat their pudding in their own room or office, just as their masters and mistresses would move to the withdrawing rooms. From the sixteenth century onwards the party would retire to the withdrawing room for tea and dessert. I suppose this developed into the custom of the men staying in the dining room to discuss the greater issues of the day and to smoke. Nowadays people nearly always stay in the dining room instead of breaking up conversations. Perhaps there should be a revival of this delightful custom of eating dessert in the withdrawing room.

Anne-Marie Stehlin's Compôte of Figs

Serves 4   Preparation time: 10 minutes   Cooking time: 10 minutes

I met this very elegant French woman years ago and amongst other subjects we talked about food. She suggested this recipe that I have used many times. I never saw her again.

2 glasses red wine
1 glass water
225g/8oz sugar
24 black figs or more, peeled
275ml/¹/₂ pint double cream,
   whipped
Brandy (optional)

1 Using a saucepan, make a syrup with the wine, water and sugar. When the sugar dissolves, boil until thickened.

2 Poach some peeled black figs for five minutes and allow to cool. Lift out the figs and reduce the liquid by half, then add some brandy to taste if desired.

Serving suggestion: Arrange the figs, halved, in a glass bowl and pour on the syrup. Serve with thick cream. The compote is best well chilled.

Surprise au Grand Marnier

Serves 6   Preparation time: 30 minutes

This is a recipe from my Tante Marie days. Usually I substitute Grand Marnier for the brandy and sherry. Other people have this recipe but I am certain this is the best one. It's not worth doing if you have spent all the housekeeping!

5 eggs, separated
75g/3oz caster sugar
1 glass brandy
1 glass sherry
1 tablespoon lemon juice
25g/1oz gelatine, softened in hot
*   water*
275ml/½ pint double cream,
*   whipped*
6 meringue shells, crushed
1 tablespoon Grand Marnier
Crystallised violets

1 Beat the yolks and sugar together. Stir in the brandy, sherry and lemon juice and add the gelatine.

2 Place a buttered jam-jar in the centre of a 20cm/8in soufflé dish and pour the mixture around the outside of the jar. Chill.

3 When the mousse has set, twist the jar out, and fill the hole with roughly crushed meringue shells. Just before serving pour the Grand Marnier over the shells and pipe some cream over the centre. Scatter the top with crystallised violets.

Figs, Raspberries and Cream

Serves 4   Preparation time: 20 minutes

Figs are my favourite fruit. When we moved here there was a fig tree in the corner of what is now my herb garden and my husband cut it down. There were terrible altercations. However, as it was only green figs I did not mourn too long.

24 black figs, or as many as desired
275ml/½ pint raspberry purée
150ml/¼ pint cream, beaten with
   some sugar or icing sugar

1 Peel and halve the figs. Arrange them in a pretty flat bowl and keep them chilled.

2 Mix the purée and the cream in equal proportions and pour over the figs. Pour the remaining purée around the edge of the dish.

Serving suggestion: Serve chilled.

A Grand Soufflé

Serves 6   Preparation time: 30 minutes   Cooking time: 20 minutes

When this was 'created' it was supposed to be Baked Alaska. I forgot to buy the ice-cream and so hustled up the soufflé on top instead. Much better — it nearly blew our heads off! This can be prepared in advance and left in the refrigerator for about 1 hour until you need to bake it.

Brandy
1 sponge cake
225g/8oz cherries, stoned
Soufflé Rothschild (see page 126)
Cream to serve

1 Soak the sponge cake in brandy until soggy and use it to line a 20cm/8in soufflé dish.

2 Spoon on to the top the Soufflé Rothschild.

Serving suggestion: Serve immediately with cream.

Soufflé Rothschild

Serves 6   Preparation time: 30 minutes   Cooking time: 20 minutes

A classic French recipe. Soufflés are easy to make and only vary in quality through lack of practice. They sink if there is a time lag between oven and table, so be very quick.

25g/1oz butter ⎱ *for the soufflé*
25g/1oz sugar ⎰   *dish*
50g/2oz butter
50g/2oz plain flour
275ml/¹/₂ pint milk, boiled
  with a vanilla pod
75g/3oz caster sugar
3 egg-yolks, beaten
4 egg-whites
150g/5oz crystallised fruits
  soaked in 1 glass Kirsch
6 strawberries rolled in caster
  sugar
Cream to serve

Pre-heat the oven to 200°C/400°F/Gas Mark 4.

1 Butter and sugar a 20cm/8in soufflé dish.

2 Melt the butter, add the flour and stir well. Pour on the hot milk, stir until thickened and boil for 5 minutes to eliminate the floury taste. Add sugar. Remove and beat in the egg-yolks.

3 Allow to cool and fold in the stiffly whisked egg whites.

4 Layer the soufflé mixture alternately with the fruits.

5 Bake in the oven at 200°C/400°F/Gas Mark 6 for 20 minutes until risen and golden. A few minutes before the end of cooking, throw in the strawberries.

Serving suggestion: Serve immediately with cream.

Chocolate Meringue Bombe

Serves 6   Preparation time: 20 minutes   Cooking time: 5 minutes   Freezing
time: Overnight

12 or more meringue shells
275ml/½ pint double cream,
  whipped
Brandy, or Grand Marnier, or an
  orange liqueur
175g/6oz chocolate menier
6 tablespoons water

1 Roughly crush the meringue shells. Whisk the cream and liqueur. Fold
  together the cream and meringue and put into an oblong plastic box,
  approximately 15cm/6in × 7.5cm/3in. Leave overnight in the freezer.

2 Before turning out of the mould, melt the chocolate and water in a bowl over
  boiling water. When melted, allow to cool and then pour over the meringue.
  Allow to set. Run a knife along the outsides and turn out.

Serving suggestion: Cut into slices to serve.

Oranges in Kirsch

Serves 6   Preparation time: 30 minutes   Cooking time: 2 minutes

I always serve this as an alternative 'slimmer's' pud, but people generally have a bit of everything offered.

10 oranges
Kirsch

1 Thinly peel the outer skin from three oranges. Chop it into matchstick lengths and blanch by boiling in some water for 2 minutes.

2 Cut the pith from oranges until you are left with a rounded shape and no inner skin or membrane.

3 Slice the oranges thinly across so that they fall into circles. Arrange in a glass bowl with the blanched orange peel and add a liberal quantity of kirsch.

Serving suggestion: Serve chilled.

Bill's Bowl of Strawberries

Makes 4–6   Preparation time: 20 minutes   Standing time: 1 day

Bill has a theory that most modern varieties of strawberry are rather tasteless and unlike those of his childhood. His method is delicious. Unlike him, however, I would use freshly squeezed limes or lemons handed round separately, instead of cream. This is more healthy and really gives the strawberries more flavour.

700g/2lb strawberries
Icing sugar
Cream or 4 limes, freshly squeezed

1 Hull the strawberries. Either halve the fruit or lightly crush them with a fork so that the juices run.

2 Sprinkle each layer liberally with seived icing sugar.

3 Leave them in a bowl in a cool place for *at least a day*. This allows them to ferment and thus give more flavour.

Serving suggestion: Hand round the lime juice or cream separately.

Plums in a Jar

Preparation time: *see* note

Very useful for the store cupboard and a real country house speciality. In fact I always use morello cherries for this recipe because they grow on a wall here. After a fairly ordinary supper of, say, left-overs, I fetch a jar from the larder as a treat. Having matured they will have become a glorious deep red colour and extremely intoxicating!

Victoria plums, damsons or cherries
Brown sugar
Brandy

1 Wash the fruit and prick with a silver fork all over.

2 Fill old jam-jars with alternate layers of fruit and brown sugar. Be generous with the sugar.

3 Pour on the brandy and fill to cover the fruit, almost to the top of the jar. Seal the jar with a lid.

Serving suggestion: Serve with thick cream.

Note: Leave for six months before eating.

Chocolate Flatlet

Serves 10   Preparation time: 40 minutes   Cooking time: 20 minutes

I made this for the first time for the dinner party after our son Thomas's christening celebrations. It would be impossible to make this as a roulade since the filling would ooze everywhere. This tastes even better after standing for a day, when everything has seeped together and has become soggy.

For the base:
6 eggs
225g/8oz caster sugar
50g/2oz cocoa

For the filling:
425ml/³⁄₄ pint double cream,
  whipped
225g/8oz raspberries steeped in
  brandy
225g/8oz chestnuts, beaten with
  sugar to taste

Pre-heat the oven to 180°C/350°F/Gas Mark 4.

---

1 Separate the egg-yolks from the whites. Beat the yolks, sugar and cocoa together. Whisk the whites until stiff and forming peaks and fold into the chocolate mixture.

---

2 Pour into a 30cm/12in × 20cm/8in tin, lined with a 7cm/3in deep Bakewell paper case. Bake at 180°C/350°F/Gas Mark 4 for 20 minutes only.

---

3 Allow to cool and cut into 3 pieces, crossways.

---

4 Layer the raspberries, cream and chestnuts with the cake, finishing with the cake.

Serving suggestion: Dust the top with icing sugar and allow everything to ooze everywhere!

Apple Crack

Serves 4   Preparation time: 5 or 15 minutes   Cooking time: 5 minutes

I remember the appley attics of my childhood – dim and warm, with dust-filled sunlight and racks of apples, with the occasional brown, dead apple adding an intoxicating smell of cider. Now in autumn we wrap apples in newspapers (do not use windfalls) and they keep until New Year. Alternatively, you can cook and purée them and store them in the freezer in 1lb bags. You could stew and purée some apples for this recipe or buy a jar of apple purée – either way this is a fairly instant pudding.

450g/1lb apples, cooked and puréed
Caster sugar
Cream to serve

---

1 Put the puréed apple into a shallow fireproof dish and cover with 0.5cm/¼in layer of sugar. Leave to stand for 20 minutes so that the sugar becomes damp.

---

2 Place the dish under the grill so that the sugar caramelises and turns dark rich brown. Leave in a cool place to allow the sugar to set.

Serving suggestion: Serve with cream.

Iced Pears and Passion-Fruit

Serves 6–8   Preparation time: 10 minutes

All the ingredients should be in your store cupboard, and I have often substituted ice-cream from the freezer if I have no cream.

700g/2lb tin of pears
3 tablespoons of any liqueur
12 passion-fruit
575ml/1 pint double cream,
  whipped lightly
50g/2oz flaked almonds

1 Strain the pears, purée in the blender or pass through a sieve. Add the liqueur to taste.

2 Add the scooped contents of the passion fruit and stir in the cream.

3 Pour into small, pretty containers and chill for at least 3 hours. Scatter the almonds over the top.

Serving suggestion: Hand round the almond biscuits separately.

Kissel

Serves 6   Preparation time: 20 minutes   Cooking time: 5 minutes

This could follow a very rich main course and it is a glorious colour.

450g/1lb redcurrants and black
  currants
450g/1lb cherries, stoned
275ml/½ pint red wine
100g/4oz sugar
1 tablespoon cornflour
50g/2oz flaked almonds
Cream to serve

1 Soften the fruits in the wine and sugar over a low heat. Thicken with cornflour and allow to cool.

2 Put into a glass bowl and scatter the top with flaked almonds. Chill.

Serving suggestion: Serve with cream and slices of damp almond cake (*see* opposite) handed round separately.

Damp Almond Cake

Serves 8   Preparation time: 15 minutes   Cooking time: 45 minutes

Sometimes the mixture curdles but this doesn't seem to make any difference to the finished cake which should be heavy and damp.

100g/4oz butter
150g/5oz caster sugar
3 eggs
100g/4oz ground almonds
40g/1½oz plain flour
2 tablespoons kirsch
Caster sugar to dust

Pre-heat the oven to 180°C/350°F/Gas Mark 4.

1 Cream the butter and the sugar. Beat in the eggs one by one, alternating with the almonds.

2 Fold in the flour with the kirsch. Spoon into a 20cm/8in × 10cm/4in loaf tin and bake for 45 minutes at 180°C/350°F/Gas Mark 4.

3 When cool, turn out and dust with sugar. Allow to cool completely on a wire rack.

Serving suggestion: This is perfect with Kissel (*see* opposite).

Crème Asphodèle

Makes 6   Preparation time: 20 minutes

This was the first pudding I learned to make at Tante Marie. It should not set like a mousse, but be slightly soft as the name 'crème' suggests.

3 eggs
165g/5½oz caster sugar
3 lemons
25g/1oz gelatine, softened in hot
   water
Cream to serve

1 Separate the eggs. Beat the sugar and yolks together and add the grated rind and juice of the lemons. Mix in the softened gelatine.

2 When the mixture starts to set and is of a custardy consistency, beat the egg-whites until stiff and fold them into the lemon mixture. Pour into a glass bowl.

Serving suggestion: Serve with cream.

Petits Pots de Chocolat au Rhum

Serves 6   Preparation time: 30 minutes   Cooking time: 5 minutes

This was the second pudding I learned to make at Tante Marie. It freezes very well.

175g/6oz chocolate menier
40g/1½oz butter
2 eggs, separated
2 generous tablespoons of rum
Cream to serve

1 Melt the chocolate in a bowl over a saucepan of boiling water. When melted, remove from the heat and put several knobs of butter on the top to melt.

2 When the mixture is cool, stir in the beaten egg-yolks and rum. Beat the whites stiffly and fold in. Pour into small pots.

Serving suggestion: Serve with cream.

Chocolate Soufflé

Serves 4   Preparation time: 20 minutes   Cooking time: 25 minutes

Well worth trying because everyone is so appreciative of a soufflé and it is not difficult to make.

Butter
25g/1oz sugar
100g/4oz plain chocolate menier
4 eggs, separated
75g/3oz caster sugar
40g/1½oz plain flour
275ml/½ pint milk, heated
Cream to serve

Pre-heat the oven to 190°C/375°F/Gas Mark 5.

1 Butter and sugar a soufflé dish. Melt the chocolate in a bowl over a pan of hot water.

2 Mix the melted chocolate, beaten egg-yolks and sugar and flour together. Pour on the heated milk.

3 Stir over a gentle heat until the mixture thickens. Whisk the egg-whites until stiff and fold into the chocolate mixture. Place in the soufflé dish in the middle of the oven at 190°C/375°F/Gas Mark 5 for 25 minutes.

Serving suggestion: Serve immediately with cream.

Compôte of Fruits

Serves 4   Preparation time: 15 minutes   Cooking time: 3 minutes

A healthy late summer pudding which might follow a rich main course. I grow all these in my garden and often eat a cômpote for breakfast.

225g/8oz each of redcurrants and
   blackcurrants
3 tablespoons soft brown sugar
225g/8oz raspberries
100g/14oz cherries, stoned
200ml/7fl oz cream, thick or
   double
200ml/7fl oz yoghurt
Soft brown sugar to serve

1 Wash the redcurrants and blackcurrants – the water clinging to them will be all you need to cook them in.

2 Put the redcurrants, blackcurrants and sugar into a pan over the heat and stir until the sugar dissolves. Try not to let the fruit split. Remove from the pan immediately.

3 Add the raspberries and stoned cherries and allow all the fruit to cool. Pour into a glass bowl.

Serving suggestion: Mix equal quantities of yoghurt and cream together and pour into a shallow dish. Cover with a liberal topping of brown sugar.

Baked Stuffed Peaches

Serves 4   Preparation time: 15 minutes   Cooking time: 20 minutes

Do not be tempted to use tinned peaches – the flavour will not equal that of fresh peaches.

6 large ripe peaches
2 level tablespoons caster sugar
25g/1oz unsalted butter
1 egg-yolk
50g/2oz amaretti or ratafia
  biscuits
Cream to serve

Pre-heat the oven to 180°C/350°F/Gas Mark 4.

1 Cut peaches in half and stone them. Enlarge the cavities with a teaspoon.

2 Mash the sugar, butter, egg-yolk and biscuits together and pile into the peaches. Place in an oven-to-table dish to facilitate serving.

3 Bake at 180°C/350°F/Gas Mark 4 until the filling is cooked, about 20 minutes.

Serving suggestion: Serve hot with cream.

Louise's Poached Pears

Serves 6   Preparation time: 10 minutes   Cooking time: 20 minutes

This is a very pretty pudding to follow a rich main course.

9 pears
1 bottle cheap red wine
100g/4oz sugar
Cinnamon stick
Cream to serve

1   Choose beautifully shaped pears and peel them, leaving the stalks on because they look prettier.

2   Place them in a large saucepan, pour over the wine, add the sugar and the cinnamon stick and heat. When the pears are cooked and looking a good pink colour on the outside, remove them to an attractive glass bowl.

3   Boil the remaining red wine until it has reduced and become slightly syrupy. Allow to cool and pour over the pears.

Serving suggestion: Chill and serve with thick cream.

Caramelised Cox's

Serves 8   Preparation time: 20 minutes   Cooking time: 35 minutes

The idea for making this evolved from eating upside-down apple tart or 'les demoiselles tatin', as named by the French. Did some demoiselles have an accident with their flan, dropping it on the floor and, unable to present it as usual, invent the upside-down apple tart? Although quite sweet, the burnt sugar topping balances the taste. I often serve this after roast meat or a plain main course.

2kg/5lb Cox's, peeled, cored and
*   sliced*
100g/4oz granulated sugar
100g/4oz butter, melted
Icing sugar
Cream to serve

Pre-heat the oven to 200°C/400°F/Gas Mark 6.

1 Mix the apples, which now weigh about 1kg/2½lb, with the sugar, stirring well so that the pieces are well coated.

2 Coat the bottom of a large, shallow heatproof dish (approximately 25cm/10in in diameter) with one tablespoon butter. Put in half the apple pieces and pour some melted butter on top. Finish with the remaining apples and butter and squash the apple pieces down.

3 Bake in an oven at 200°C/400°F/Gas Mark 6 for 30 minutes.

4 Remove from the oven and drain the juices into a saucepan. Boil rapidly until the liquid reduces and becomes syrupy. Pour over the apples. Cover with a thick layer of icing sugar and put under a grill until the sugar has caramelised and is dark brown.

Serving suggestion: Serve warm or cold.

Bombe Savernake

An enormous and ancient mulberry tree grows on the side of our house. The fruit is terribly difficult to pick owing to the dense foliage, and so everyone avoids picking it. I have copied the Greek peasants and spread a sheet underneath to catch the fruit, just as they do for the olives. It is almost black and overripe when it finally falls from the tree.

12 large meringue shells
275ml/½ pint double cream,
  whipped
Raspberry liqueur
350g/12oz mulberries

1 Roughly crush the meringue shells. Mix the cream and liqueur to taste and fold on to the shells. Stir in about 20 mulberries. Pile the mixture into any plastic container and freeze overnight.

2 Purée and sieve the remaining mulberries.

Serving suggestion: When you are ready to serve this pudding, scoop out the mixture into small bowls or plates and pour some purée on to each.

Sunken Strawberries

Makes 8–10   Preparation time: 30 minutes

Try to buy wild strawberries or Alpines because they taste better. I grow them in my garden and they spread very readily. However, members of the family seem to eat them as they pass, so I never have enough to pick and often resort to buying. This dish is simple to make but rich and requires no cooking at all.

75g/3oz caster sugar
275ml/½ pint double cream,
*   whipped, or fromage blanc*
1.5kg/3lb strawberries, washed
*   and hulled*
4 tablespoons curaçao
4 tablespoons rum (or more to
*   taste)*
Crystallised rose petals and
*   violets to decorate*

1 Mix together the caster sugar and whipped cream.

2 Add all the other ingredients and mix well.

Serving suggestion: Decorate with crystallised rose petals and violets.

Crêpes

I make a batch of crêpes in advance, layer them with greaseproof paper, put them into a plastic bag and freeze them until required. Some people freeze them with fillings but some of the following recipes would not be suitable for this. On the day they are needed I make the sauce or filling while the crêpes are defrosting, fill the crêpes and arrange them on the dish that I will be using. I can then cover them with some buttered greaseproof paper and reheat them at the same time as I cook the vegetables for dinner.

150g/5oz plain flour
1 egg and 1 extra yolk
1 tablespoon olive oil
275ml/½ pint milk
Extra oil for frying
Extra milk

1 Sieve the flour into a bowl, make a well in the centre, pour in the egg and egg-yolk, oil and some milk. Whisk in the rest of the milk by degrees. Alternatively, put all the ingredients in the liquidiser.

2 Heat some olive oil in a flat-bottomed iron pan (15cm/6in in diameter) and pour off the excess. Pour in enough batter to cover the surface very thinly. (Add some milk to the pancake mixture if it seems too thick). When the edges bubble, loosen with a spatula and either toss the crêpe or turn it with the spatula. Discard the first crêpe.

Serving suggestion: *See* the following recipes.

Note: The crêpes can be kept hot by putting on an upturned cereal bowl and placing in a colander over hot water.

Crêpes Suzette

Serves 6   Preparation time: 20 minutes

This famous and classic dish is most people's idea of flamboyance and a cliché similar to 'kiss me quick' hats. However, don't be put off – it is easy to make and very delicious.

12 crêpes (see page 145)
2 oranges
100g/4oz sugar
100g/4oz butter, softened
4 tablespoons curaçao
Finish with 4 tablespoons brandy
  and some icing sugar

---

1 Peel the oranges very thinly. Chop the rind finely with half the sugar.

---

2 Beat the softened butter until fluffy. Add the orange skin, sugar and curaçao.

---

3 Spread on to each pancake and fold into four.

---

4 Put on a hot, buttered dish and dust the tops with icing sugar.

Serving suggestion: Warm the brandy, pour it over and set alight just before serving.

Crêpes Stuffed with Cherries

Serves 6   Preparation time: 5 minutes   Cooking time: 10 minutes

12 crêpes (see page 145)
450g/1lb stoned black cherries,
  tinned
50g/2oz cornflour
Brandy
275ml/½ pint double cream,
  whipped
50g/2oz flaked almonds

Pre-heat the oven to 200°C/400°F/Gas Mark 6.

1 Sieve the cherries and reserve the syrup in the tin. Thicken the juice with the
  cornflour and add the cherries and some brandy to taste.

2 Put a little of the mixture on each pancake and roll up. It's all the better if the
  cherries ooze out of the ends!

3 Place in an ovenproof oval dish and cover with greaseproof paper. Heat in the
  oven for 5 minutes at 200°C/400°F/Gas Mark 6 before serving.

Serving suggestion: Put spoonfuls of whipped cream on top of each
pancake and scatter on the flaked almonds.

Note: This and the following crêpe filling recipes can be made in advance
and put together at the last minute to be reheated in the oven at 200°C/400°F/
Gas Mark 6. It is imperative that the dish is well covered and sealed with
greaseproof paper so that the edges do not become crisp.

Crêpes Stuffed with Pears

Serves 6   Preparation time: 20 minutes   Cooking time: 5 minutes

12 crêpes (see page 145)
400g/14oz tin pears, puréed
2 tablespoons Cointreau
3 egg-whites
3 tablespoons caster sugar
Crystallised violets to decorate

Pre-heat the oven to 200°C/400°F/Gas Mark 6.

1 Mix the Cointreau with the pear purée and spread equally on all the crêpes.
   Fold each crêpe to form a triangle.

2 Arrange in an ovenproof dish.

3 Whip the egg-whites until they are stiff, fold in the sugar and spread the
   meringue over the pancakes. Scatter some violets on top. Bake in the oven at
   200°C/400°F/Gas Mark 6 for 5 minutes or until golden.

Serving suggestion: Decorate with crystallised violets before serving.

Crêpes Normandes

Serves 6   Preparation time: 20 minutes   Cooking time: 10 minutes

12 crêpes (see page 145)
700g/2lb Cox's, peeled and sliced
100g/4oz unsalted butter
4 tablespoons soft brown sugar
275ml/½ pint double cream,
*   whipped*
150ml/¼ pint Calvados, plus 4
*   tablespoons Calvados to flame*
Icing sugar

1 Cook the apples in butter and sugar until they are soft and purée in a blender or pass through a vegetable mill.

2 Mix the cream and Calvados. Layer the mixture with the crêpes to resemble a cake. Dust the top with sieved icing sugar. Heat 4 more tablespoons of Calvados and set alight.

Serving suggestion: Keep all the ingredients warm and put them together at the last minute. Cut in slices as you would for a cake.

Pear Feuilleté

Serves 8   Preparation time: 20 minutes   Cooking time: 15 minutes

Reasonably simple to make, you could substitute Fillo pastry. This is light and refreshing after a rich main course and it looks pretty enough to give the impression you've spent hours creating it!

4 large pears, peeled, cored and
   sliced lengthwise
1 glass white wine
½ glass water
100g/4oz sugar
225g/8oz rough puff pastry
Beaten egg
275ml/½ pint raspberry purée,
   sieved
275ml/½ pint single cream
Angelica

Pre-heat the oven to 200°C/400°F/Gas Mark 6.

---

1 Poach the pears in the wine, water and sugar. Lift them out, drain them and allow to cool.

---

2 Meanwhile cut the pastry into 8 oblong shapes which are big enough to lie the pears on them lengthwise. Brush with beaten egg and bake for 10 minutes at 200°C/400°F/Gas Mark 6.

---

3 Pour the raspberry purée on to individual dessert plates, place the cooled pastry in the middle with the pear on top.

Serving suggestion: Dribble and squiggle the cream over the fruit and decorate each with a diamond of angelica.

Crème Brûlée

Serves 6–8   Preparation time: 5 minutes   Cooking time: 10 minutes   Chilling time: Overnight

This is an extremely rich dish and should follow a grilled or roasted main course. I nearly always serve some puréed fruit or a compote of red and black currants from the freezer with it. Served separately, your guests can spoon it on top if they wish.

6 egg-yolks
50g/2oz sugar
850ml/1½ pints double cream
Vanilla essence
6 heaped tablespoons caster sugar

1 Mix the egg-yolks with the sugar. Heat the cream almost to scalding point with a drop of vanilla essence and pour over the eggs. Strain the mixture into a clean pan. Stir gradually and allow to thicken over the heat. Do not allow the cream to boil or it will curdle.

2 Pour the mixture into 6 ramekins and leave to cool in the refrigerator for at least 6 hours, and preferably overnight.

3 Cover the tops of the ramekins with 6 heaped tablespoons of caster sugar and place under a pre-heated grill so that the sugar melts and turns to caramel.

4 Remove from the grill and leave in a cool place. Do not place in the refrigerator or the caramel will soften.

Serving suggestion: Serve with puréed fruit or a compote.

Crème Caramel

Serves 8   Preparation time: 10 minutes   Cooking time: 25 minutes

Many people confuse the ingredients of this and crème Brulée and have been known to bake, cream and thicken the milk mercilessly. At Tante Marie we made these bases for various elaborate desserts. These were piled high with fruits and piped with stars to resemble Victorian illustrations for Mrs Beaton's cookbook. However, I prefer them to be very simple and somehow they seem to aid digestion after a rich meal.

For the caramel
100g/4oz sugar
75ml/3fl oz water

For the crème:
3 eggs
4 egg-yolks
150g/6oz sugar
575ml/1 pint milk, heated
275ml/½ pint double cream

Pre-heat the oven to 180°C/350°F/Gas Mark 4.

1 First make the caramel by boiling the sugar and water rapidly until the sugar starts to turn brown. Pour immediately into ramekins.

2 For the crème, beat the eggs and egg-yolks with the sugar. Pour on the hot milk, mixing well. Strain and pour into the ramekins. Place all the ramekins in a roasting tin filled with warm water. Bake for 20 minutes, or until set, at 180°C/350°F/Gas Mark 4.

3 Allow to cool before unmoulding on to individual plates. Sometimes the top of the custard has to be loosened with a knife, but usually they will fall out easily.

Serving suggestion: Sometimes I pour puréed fruit with a little kirsch over the unmoulded crèmes.

CHAPTER 9

QUICK AND RICH DESSERTS

Fruit Fools	154
Mille Feuilles	155
Peach Brûlée Astor	156
Peach or Raspberry Brûlée Weldon	157
Sigrid's Peaches	158
Marrons et Pommes	159
Chestnuts, Gooseberries and Cream	160
Bombe Alaska	161
Elizabethan Lemon Posset	162
Alexandra's Grape Brûlée	163

This assortment of quick and rich puddings are good as stand-bys. Almost all the ingredients can be found in a well-stocked larder and thick cream can be frozen and defrosted easily and quickly. They should follow grilled meat or fish dishes and, however lazy you feel about the entire dinner or lunch, these guarantee to give an air of effort and gastronomic style. I have learned many quick tricks, including recipes which don't need exactly measured quantities of ingredients and I hope these will be of help to anyone in a rush. For example, raisins soaked in rum or grapes soaked in Pernod can be folded into or poured over ice-cream to give an elegant and speedy dessert. Tinned peaches can be blended with ratafia biscuits with a little Cointreau added to taste. The mixture should be spooned into small glasses and topped with a ratafia biscuit. Similarly, buy large brandy snaps and fill the ends with cream, or place scoops of ice-cream on to puréed soft fruit and pour thick cream on top which will set on contact with the ice. You can make up all these recipes according to your own tastes and requirements.

Fruit Fools

Serves 6   Preparation time: 20 minutes

I often use mulberries because we have an enormous tree growing up the side of our house. By the time they ripen they are too soft and black to use for anything else. I use mulberry leaves to decorate all the fools.

900g/2½lb raspberries,
    blackcurrants, gooseberries,
    blackberries or mulberries
Soft brown sugar
275ml/½ pint Devon clotted cream
    or double cream, whipped
Almond biscuits or macaroons

---

1 If you use gooseberries it may be necessary to cook them. Wash them and use the water clinging to their skins to cook them in a pan with the sugar. Stir all the time until the fruit starts to split and the sugar dissolves. Allow to cool.

---

2 Purée the fruit of your choice, reserving 8oz fruit to be used whole. Reserve about 3 tablespoons of the purée for decoration. Mix most of the puréed fruit and all the reserved whole fruit with the cream and pour into a glass bowl. Decorate with some swirls or zigzags of the reserved purée. Chill before serving.

Serving suggestion: Hand round a plate of almond biscuits or macaroons separately.

Mille Feuilles

Makes 8–10   Preparation time: 20 minutes   Cooking time: 10 minutes

This is astonishingly easy and everyone imagines you have been baking for hours.

450g/1lb puff pastry
450g/1lb raspberry perserve
275ml/½ pint double cream
Icing sugar

Pre-heat the oven to 200°C/400°F/Gas Mark 6.

---

1 Roll out the pastry and cut into thick round or oblong shapes with a pastry cutter. Bake in the oven at 200°C/400°F/Gas Mark 6 until golden (10 minutes).

---

2 Split each piece of pastry into three layers. Spread each layer with the preserve and cream. Sandwich the layers back together.

Serving suggestion: Dust the tops with icing sugar before serving.

Peach Brûlée Astor

Serves 6   Preparation time: 15 minutes   Cooking time: 25 minutes   Chilling time: Overnight

Although rich this is much more subtle than the slightly easier method on page 157. Use a good quality double cream, possibly unpasteurised; if stirred very carefully it is unlikely to curdle.

4 egg-yolks
1 tablespoon caster sugar
575ml/1 pint double cream
A few drops vanilla essence
6 peaches, peeled and sliced
Caster sugar for the topping

1 Beat the yolks and sugar together in a bowl. Heat the cream with the vanilla essence in a saucepan to just below scalding and then pour on to the yolks, stirring well.

2 Pour the mixture through a sieve into a bowl over boiling water (a double boiler). Stir well until the cream thickens. I never use a double boiler but risk my all with a saucepan over the heat. By removing the saucepan several times from the heat and stirring vigorously you can prevent curdling. I don't advise this unless you are very confident. Make sure that the saucepan is well rinsed.

3 Pour the cream on to the peaches arranged in an oven-proof fish. Chill overnight.

4 Cover the cream with a thick layer of caster sugar and grill until the sugar caramelises.

Serving suggestion: Leave in a cool place until needed.

Peach or Raspberry Brûlée Weldon

Serves 8   Preparation time: 15 minutes   Cooking time: 5 minutes   Chilling time: Overnight

The first time I had this with raspberries I exclaimed how delicious it was. My hostess Mandy said she thought everyone knew the method. It all turns into a wonderful bubbly mess of sugar and cream, and tastes delicious.

8 peaches or 575g/1½lb raspberries
575ml/1 pint double cream,
  whipped
Soft brown sugar

1 Peel the peaches and slice them fairly thinly. Arrange them in an ovenproof dish and cover with the cream. If you are using raspberries mix them together with the cream and place them in an ovenproof dish in the same way.

2 Leave in the refrigerator for several hours or overnight.

3 Cover the mixture with the soft brown sugar and grill for 5 minutes or so until most of the sugar is caramelised.

Serving suggestion: Leave in a cool place until needed.

Sigrid's Peaches

Serves 6   Preparation time: 15 minutes   Cooking time: 15 minutes

The time spent on this is worth the effort. Tinned peaches do not taste as good as fresh in this recipe.

9 peaches, peeled and sliced
175g/6oz soft brown sugar
Cinnamon
Crème fraîche to serve

Pre-heat the oven to 200°C/400°F/Gas Mark 6.

1   Arrange the sliced peaches in a shallow baking dish. Mix the sugar and cinnamon to taste and cover the peaches.

2   Bake for 15 minutes at 200°C/400°F/Gas Mark 6 until the sugar has melted and forms bubbles.

Serving suggestion: Allow to cool slightly and serve with crème fraîche, which is readily available in good supermarkets and delicatessens.

Marrons et Pommes

Serves 8   Preparation time: 10 minutes

All these ingredients are easily available from larder or freezer.

400g/14oz jar apple purée
225g/8oz tin chestnut purée
Sugar to taste
Cointreau
375ml/12fl oz double cream,
 whipped
100g/4oz tin marrons glacés

1 Mix the apple and chestnut purée together and add the sugar and Cointreau to taste.

2 Fold the mixture into the whipped cream and pour into a glass bowl. Decorate with pieces of marrons glacés.

Serving suggestion: Serve chilled.

Chestnuts, Gooseberries and Cream

Serves 6   Preparation time: 10 minutes

A gooseberry fool with a difference!

400g/14oz tin gooseberries
225g/8oz tin chestnut purée
Caster sugar
275ml/10fl oz double cream
100g/4oz chocolate menier or dark
    chocolate
Amaretto biscuits or macaroons to
    serve

1 Purée the gooseberries and add to the chestnut purée. Add some sugar to taste.

2 Whip the cream until thick and mix with the purées. Pour into a glass bowl. Scatter the grated chocolate over the top and chill.

Serving suggestion: Serve with Amaretto biscuits, which may be bought at most delicatessens.

Bombe Alaska

Serves 6   Preparation time: 10 minutes   Cooking time: 5 minutes

A cliché pudding but very quick and festive!

Large sponge cake
Ice-cream block (family size)
225g/8oz pitted cherries
150ml/¼ pint brandy
4 egg-whites
1 tablespoon caster sugar

Pre-heat the oven to 220°C/425°F/Gas Mark 7.

---

1 Shape the sponge to a square or oblong (this makes it easier to cut later on). Place on a large ovenproof dish. Soak the cherries in the brandy and then drain. Pour the brandy over the sponge. Spread with a layer of ice-cream and sprinkle the cherries over the top.

---

2 Whip the egg-whites until stiff, fold in the sugar and spread all over the ice-cream to completely cover and seal. Bake in a hot oven 220°C/425°F/Gas Mark 7 for about 5 minutes until slightly set and just beginning to brown.

Serving suggestion: Serve at once.

Elizabethan Lemon Posset

Serves 6   Preparation time: 10 minutes

Syllabub to the rest of us! You can use brandy and sherry if you have no Madeira.

Juice and grated rind of 3 lemons
4 tablespoons caster sugar
575ml/1 pint double cream
1 glass Madeira, or to taste
Grated nutmeg
Amaretto biscuits or macaroons

1 Soak the grated lemon rind in the lemon juice and sugar.

2 Whip the cream to a stiff consistency. Fold the Madeira and lemon mixture carefully into the cream. Beat the cream again until it is stiff once more.

Serving suggestion: Serve in an attractive glass bowl with some grated nutmeg sprinkled on the top. Hand round the biscuits separately.

Alexandra's Grape Brûlée

Serves 6   Preparation time: 5 minutes   Cooking time: 5 minutes   Chilling time: Overnight

This recipe can be made with many different fruits – one delicious alternative is raspberries. Sometimes I use cream by itself or Greek yoghurt by itself. I always use unpasteurised, thick cream that is at least a day old because it seems to mature and become extremely thick and there is no need to whip.

275ml/½ pint double cream
275ml/½ pint Greek yoghurt
450g/1lb Muscat grapes
Soft brown sugar

1 Stir the cream and yoghurt together and mix with the grapes. Put the mixture into an ovenproof dish and chill overnight.

2 Cover the mixture with a thick layer of sugar and put under the grill until the sugar melts, bubbles and forms a crust.

Serving suggestion: Leave in a cool place for a few hours before serving.

CHAPTER 10

TEA-TIME

Shooting Fruit Cake	165
Glaçage au Chocolat	166
Chocolate Treacle Cake	167
Thin Gidgers	168
Banana and Date Loaf	169
Granny's Bread	170
Reine de Saba	171

Probably because of the children, tea-time has become something of an institution in our household. We have home-made bread thickly cut and spread with honey or home-made jam. Both bread and scones freeze well and although I prefer bread to defrost slowly, I put scones in the microwave and they warm up to become as if they had just been baked. Egg sandwiches made with the addition of some mayonnaise, or cucumber and Marmite or tomato sandwiches, well peppered, are some of our favourites. They take very little time to prepare and friends regard our teas as old-fashioned and a treat.

I keep several varieties of leaf tea in my cupboard and favour Lapsang Souchong or Keemun. I prefer to drink passion flower tea and the infusions such as camomile and peppermint in the evening after dinner. I have a small collection of teapots in varying sizes, including a favourite pot for one, and will only drink from bone china or porcelain. As a compromise we have bone-china mugs as there is nothing so dreadful as thick pottery mugs and delicate tea.

Shooting Fruit Cake

Makes 3kg/7lb cake   Preparation time: 30 minutes   Cooking time: 3¼–4 hours

An extremely rich fruit cake, I serve this instead of pudding at shoot lunches in the winter, handing round the cheese board at the same time. Try a piece of creamy Stilton or some well-matured Cheddar in the same mouthful. Pass the Madeira and Port and send your friends well fortified out into the cold. Alternatively, cut a thin slice at tea-time accompanied by some fine China tea such as Lapsang Souchong or Keemun.

6 eggs
8oz/225g caster sugar
Juice and grated rind of 1 orange
Juice and grated rind of 1 lemon
450g/1lb currants
450g/1lb sultanas
450g/1lb raisins

225g/8oz glacé cherries
225g/8oz mixed peel
225g/8oz flour
100g/4oz ground almonds
15g/½oz mixed spice
225g/8oz butter, melted
Brandy to taste

Pre-heat the oven to 130°C/250°F/Gas Mark ½.

1 Beat the eggs and sugar together.

2 Place the orange and lemon rind, dried fruit, fruit juice and mixed peel in a large mixing bowl. Stir the flour, almonds and spice into the egg mixture and add to the dried fruit. Mix thoroughly.

3 Pour the melted butter into the mixture and combine.

4 Line a large loaf tin with greaseproof paper and fill this with the mixture to within 5cm/2in of the top. Cover with an oblong of greaseproof paper. Bake for 5½ hours at 130°C/250°F/Gas Mark ½. Check regularly and if the top starts to burn, turn down the oven a little to 100°C/200°F/Gas Mark low. The cake will be cooked when the skewer comes out clean when testing.

5 When cool, spike with a skewer and pour on brandy. Wrap in silver foil and leave for several weeks.

Serving suggestion: Cut into thick slices and sprinkle on extra brandy.

Note: I once left my cakes overnight in the bottom of the Aga and they were perfect. The temperature was 130°C/250°F/Gas Mark ½.

Glaçage au Chocolat

Preparation time: 10 minutes   Cooking time: 5 minutes

This icing is suitable for many cakes and gives a delicious topping with a touch of extravagance. I recommend using good bitter chocolate because I find cooking chocolate to be rather tasteless.

75g/3oz chocolate menier or dark
* chocolate*
2 tablespoons brandy
65g/2½oz unsalted butter

1 Melt the chocolate with the brandy in a bowl over hot water. Remove from the heat and beat in the butter.

2 Spread over the cake leaving the surface fairly rough.

Serving suggestion: Use as a topping for Reine de Saba (*see* page 171).

Chocolate Treacle Cake

Makes 1 cake   Preparation time: 10 minutes   Cooking time: 20 minutes

This recipe is very quick and simple and is made without eggs.

For the cake:
50ml/2fl oz vegetable oil
2 tablespoons black treacle
225ml/8fl oz milk
25g/1oz cocoa
50g/2oz soft brown sugar
2 teaspoons bicarbonate of soda
  (heaped)
3 heaped teaspoons baking powder
1 generous tablespoon wine vinegar
1 tablespoon water
1 teaspoon vanilla essence

For the filling:
Black cherry jam
150ml/½ pint double cream,
  whipped (or crème fraîche)
Icing sugar

Pre-heat the oven to 220°C/425°F/Gas Mark 7.

1 Heat the oil, treacle and milk in a pan, mix well and cool. Pour the cooled mixture on to the dry ingredients and stir well. Add the vinegar, water and vanilla essence and combine thoroughly.

2 Pour into 2 ready-greased 18cm/7in cake tins and bake at 220°C/425°F/Gas Mark 7 for 20 minutes.

3 When the cake is cool, sandwich the 2 layers together with the jam and cream.

Serving suggestion: Dust the top with icing sugar.

Thin Gidgers

Makes 12   Preparation time: 5 minutes   Cooking time: 15 minutes

Heavenly, fudge-tasting, flap-jackish biscuits.

100g/4oz butter
100g/4oz brown sugar
1 generous tablespoon golden syrup
100g/4oz flour
100g/4oz rolled oats
1 teaspoon bicarbonate of soda

Pre-heat the oven to 180°C/350°F/Gas Mark 4.

---

1 Melt the butter and sugar, then add the syrup, flour and oats. Add the bicarbonate of soda and stir well.

---

2 Place heaped teaspoons of the mixture on to a greased baking tray leaving plenty of space between them. Bake at 180°C/350°F/Gas Mark 4 for 15 minutes until golden. Sometimes they need a little longer. Once cooked, leave to cool on a wire rack to set firm.

Serving suggestion: They can be moulded into shape whilst still warm by placing them over inverted jam-jars and allowing them to flop down the sides, when they become edible cases for superior desserts. Leave them until they are cold before using.

Banana and Date Loaf

Makes 1 loaf   Preparation time: 15 minutes   Cooking time: 45 minutes

This loaf keeps well in an airtight tin and lasts at least a week.

100g/4oz butter, softened
100g/4oz caster sugar
2 eggs
150g/6oz self-raising flour, sifted
1 teaspoon baking soda
4 bananas, roughly mashed
3 tablespoons dates

Pre-heat the oven to 200°C/400°F/Gas Mark 6.

1 Cream the butter and sugar together. Beat in the eggs. Stir in the flour together with the baking soda.

2 Add the bananas and the dates and pour the whole mixture into a large loaf tin. Cover with foil and bake for 45 minutes at 200°C/400°F/Gas Mark 6, uncovering for the last 5 minutes.

Granny's Bread

Makes 2 loaves   Preparation time: 40–50 minutes   Cooking time: 30 minutes

Bread-making has been revolutionized by modern technology in the form of dried yeast. No more hanging about all day waiting for the bread to rise only to have to beat it senseless once more for another proving. This recipe is almost foolproof but improves with each subsequent attempt. It should be slighly crusty and make a hollow sound when the base is rapped with the knuckles.

450g/1lb stoneground flour
1 sachet dried yeast
1 teaspoon salt
1 teaspoon sugar
350–425ml/12–15fl oz warm water
2 tablespoons oil

Pre-heat the oven to 200°C/400°F/Gas Mark 6.

1 Place all the dry ingredients into a bowl. Mix the oil and water in a jug. Slowly add this to the flour whilst beating to make a soft dough. (The exact amount of liquid can vary with each batch.)

2 Beat for 10 minutes by hand or 3–4 minutes in a mixer.

3 Lightly grease 2 loaf tins and half fill each one. Leave in a warm place for between 30 and 40 minutes. Bake on the bottom rack of the oven for 20–30 minutes at 200°C/400°F/Gas Mark 6. Test for readiness by knocking the base with the knuckles. If it sounds hollow then the bread is ready.

4 Turn out of the tin and 'finish' the bread by turning it upside-down in a hot oven for 1 minute, or in the same oven for 6 minutes.

Serving suggestion: Serve on its own or with butter.

Reine De Saba

Serves 8   Preparation time: 20 minutes   Cooking time: 25 minutes

This is *the* best chocolate cake in the whole world. It is slightly under-done in the middle but be brave and don't overcook, otherwise the texture is ruined. The result is a rather sophisticated cake – for grown-ups only!

150g/5oz chocolate menier
2 tablespoons brandy
100g/4oz butter, softened
100g/4oz caster sugar
4 eggs, separated
Caster sugar
Salt
75g/3oz ground almonds
¼ teaspoon almond extract
65g/2½oz plain flour, sifted
Glaçage au chocolat (see page 166)

Pre-heat the oven to 180°C/350°F/Gas Mark 4.

1 Melt the chocolate with the brandy. Cream the butter and sugar together and beat in the egg-yolks. Stir in the chocolate, almonds and almond extract.

2 Beat the egg-whites until nearly stiff. Sprinkle on 1 tablespoon of sugar and continue beating until stiff.

3 Fold the egg-whites a quarter at a time into the mixture, alternating with the sifted flour.

4 Turn the mixture into a buttered and floured 20cm/8in tin. Bake in the oven for 25 minutes at 180°C/350°F/Gas Mark 4. The cake is ready when the outer 7.5cm/3in are set and a skewer comes out clean. Allow to cool on a wire rack.

Serving suggestion: Cover the cake in glaçage au chocolat (*see* page 166).

CHAPTER 11

ACCOMPANIMENTS

Sauce Maltaise	172
Croûtes and Croûtons	172
Mayonnaise	173
Tomato Mayonnaise	173
Vinaigrette	174
Hollandaise Sauce	174
Tomato Sauce	174

Sauce Maltaise

Preparation time: 5 minutes

Hollandaise sauce (see page 174)
Juice and grated rind of 1 orange

1 Put the hollandaise sauce into a bowl and add the juice and grated rind.

2 Mix well.

Croûtes and Croûtons

Preparation time: 5 minutes   Cooking time: 5–10 minutes

White bread   *Butter*

Pre-heat the oven to 200°C/400°F/Gas Mark 6.

1 Remove the crusts from the bread and cut to the required oblong shapes, at least half an inch thick for croûtes, and into small dice shapes for croûtons.

2 Using a roasting pan, soak the bread in a generous portion of melted butter. Cook in the oven until golden.

Note: The croûtes will need to be turned once during cooking; the croûtons will need to be turned several times with a spatula or fish slice.

Mayonnaise

Preparation time: 5–10 minutes

½ teaspoon Dijon mustard
1 egg-yolk
275ml/½ pint sunflower oil
White wine vinegar or lemon juice
Salt
White pepper

1 Stir the mustard and yolk together in a bowl.

2 Drip on the oil slowly and whisk, without ceasing, until all the oil has been added. Season well.

3 Stir in the vinegar or lemon until you have the required consistency.

Note: If the mixture curdles use a new bowl and an extra egg-yolk and drip in the curdled mayonnaise slowly, whisking until thick. It will be necessary to add extra oil at the end, taking care not to curdle it all over again. Most recipes will survive the use of bottled mayonnaise.

Tomato Mayonnaise

Preparation time: 10 minutes

Use a stiff mayonnaise made with not too much vinegar.

275ml/½ pint mayonnaise (see above)
Juice of 1 lemon
1 tablespoon tarragon
1 tablespoon parsley
1 tablespoon basil
1 tablespoon tomato purée
450g/1lb tomatoes, puréed and sieved
Salt and pepper

1 Flavour the mayonnaise with the other ingredients.

2 Combine well.

Serving suggestion: This sauce goes well with the terrine of salmon (page 77).

Vinaigrette

1 teaspoon made English mustard
Salt and pepper
1 tablespoon sugar

50ml/2fl oz wine vinegar
175ml/6fl oz olive oil

1 Mix the mustard, salt, pepper, sugar and wine vinegar together.

2 Pour on the oil slowly and whisk until well mixed.

Variations: You might add: handfuls of chopped mint or chives; the mashed yolks of two hard-boiled eggs; finely chopped shallots and parsley; or some cloves of garlic, crushed. This recipe can also be made with walnut oil.

Hollandaise Sauce

2 tablespoons vegetable water
2 egg-yolks
100g/4oz butter

1 tablespoon lemon juice
Pepper

1 Beat the stock and egg-yolks in a bowl over a pan of boiling water.

2 Remove from the heat and beat in the butter by degrees, either by hand whisk or by putting all the ingredients into a liquidiser. The mixture will thicken and if it curdles put everything into the refrigerator for a few minutes. Remove and whisk or blend again. Stir in the lemon juice and season.

Tomato Sauce

Preparation time: 5 minutes   Cooking time: 35 minutes

1 large onion, chopped
25g/1oz butter
2 cloves garlic, crushed

400g/14oz tin chopped tomatoes
Oregano and basil
Salt and pepper

1 Sauté the onions in butter until soft. Add garlic and cook for 1 minute.

2 Add the tomatoes, herbs and seasoning and simmer for at least 30 minutes. Allow to stand and re-heat when needed.

GLOSSARY

Bain Marie   A large pan or roasting dish filled with boiling water which is placed in an oven. The recipe to be so cooked, e.g. Crème Caramel, is placed in a smaller ovenproof dish and this dish then placed into the bain marie where it is cooked by the effects of the steam rising from the water. This is also a good method for keeping sauces and food warm.

Beurre Manié   Soft butter and flour mashed together. This mixture is then whisked into hot soup or sauce in order to thicken it.

Bullaces   Bullaces grow wild in the hedgerows and are slightly larger than sloes. Sometimes they are confused with wild damsons. Bullace cheese might be served at the end of the meal.

Chicorée Frisée   Curly endive, lettuce with a frizzy head. It looks very pretty mixed with raddiccio.

Croûte   A square or oblong of fried bread or pastry.

Croûtons   Small cubes of fried bread used as a garnish for soups.

Fleurons   Classically a crescent shape of puff pastry cut with a crinkle-edged cutter, but it could also be a circle.

Fruit Cheese   Fruit and sugar reduced by boiling to a pulp which sets when cold. Stored in jars it keeps for several years. It is a delicious accompaniment to game and some cold meats, or secretly and sinfully spooned from the jar and eaten with thick cream! Although they can be made from almost anything, fruit cheeses are most successful using apples, crab apples or quinces as well as plums, damsons, cherries and bullaces.

Liason   A thickening for sauces and soups etc. It can be made with a mixture of egg yolks and cream, or melted butter and flour (a roux), or a beurre manié.

Liquor   These are the juices of whatever you are cooking but the term usually refers to fish. The wine and water in which fish is poached is called a fumet.

Mâche   Better known as Lamb's Lettuce, this is dark green and grows in a cluster rather like a weed.

Marinade   A liquid mixture of wine, vinegar, oil and spices used to tenderise and/or flavour fish and meat, especially venison.

Pommes de Terre Boulangère   Sliced potatoes and onions with stock, cream and plenty of fresh ground black pepper baked in a fireproof dish. The classic recipe omits cream and the potatoes and onions are layered with cheese and topped with breadcrumbs.

Radiccio   A beautiful and tiny red-and-cream coloured type of chicory resembling a lettuce.

INDEX

Anchovy fillets 47
Apples 102, 106, 117, 132
   Cox's 110, 113, 142, 149
Artichoke hearts 35, 41, 43
Avocados 26, 36, 38

Bananas 99, 111, 169
Beans 26, 28, 34, 35, 40, 47
Beetroot 19, 35
Biscuits 140, 154, 160, 162

Cauliflower 34, 35
Celeriac 35, 64
Celery 16, 17, 31, 34, 90, 95
Chestnuts 29, 131, 159, 160
Cherries 98, 109, 125, 130, 134, 139,
   147, 161, 165
Chives 42, 43, 47, 61, 70
Chocolate 119, 127, 137, 138, 160,
   166, 171
Consommé 19, 44
Courgettes 22, 28, 65
Cucumber 34, 35, 40, 70

Figs 122, 124
Fruits,
   Crystallized 106, 126
   Mixed dried 116

Ginger 87
Golden syrup 102, 104, 115, 168
Gooseberries 154, 160
Grapes, Muscat 163

Ham 23, 52, 53, 57
Hare 92

Leeks 17, 27
Liver 24, 32, 94
Lobster 68, 71

Marmalade 112, 114
Meringue shells 123, 127, 143
Mulberries 100, 143, 154
Mussels 64, 65, 69, 72

Olives 24, 25, 45, 47, 76
Oranges 68, 90, 128, 146

Pâté 24, 41
Peaches 140, 156, 157, 158
Pears 133, 141, 148, 150
Peppers, green 18, 36, 40, 44
Peppercorns 31, 77, 90, 93
Pheasant 85, 86, 87
Pigeon 29, 94, 95
Plums 98, 130
Potatoes 13, 16, 47, 95

Radiccio 29, 34, 68
Raspberries 46, 109, 131, 139, 154,
   157
Redcurrants 90, 91, 100, 109, 134, 139
Rhubarb 99
Roe, black and red lumpfish 61, 71, 73

Salmon 44, 50, 66, 73, 74, 77
Scallops 65, 76
Shallots 76, 77, 85
Spinach 15, 30
Sponge 114, 125, 129, 144
Strawberries 126, 129, 144

Trout 74, 80
Tuna 40, 47,

Walnuts 29, 45
Watercress 34, 66, 85

Yoghurt 28, 139, 163